'*Timeless Management* oozes good sense – a valuable book for managers at all levels.... It places the emphasis squarely on people and the nature of their interactions – as well as their need to feel comfortable, to belong, to understand and be valued.'
Professor Peter R. Crane FRS, *Director, Royal Botanic Gardens, Kew*

'So many of the practices of "good" management they advocate as appropriate for life in the twenty-first century are recognisable as aspects of good governance in the actions of others much earlier in history. I was also left wondering how many other businesses in the UK acted so promptly and with such vision to protect their viability and employees as has Historic Royal Palaces under Alan Coppin's leadership.'
Sir Rodney Walker, *Chairman, UK Sports Council; English National Stadium Trust; West Yorkshire Broadcasting*

'a comprehensive "primer" for managers and anyone in a leadership position – it is highly readable and accessible, almost a manual; very clearly structured, with clear "models"; and a remarkable and unusual use of historical figures. Part 3 ... is a very powerful section, describing how all this doctrine was applied to a real organisation undergoing change, and especially the post September 11th crisis. I lost count of the times I said to myself things like "Yes of course!" and "I must remember that point" and "That feels right!"'
David Quarmby, *Chairman, British Tourist Authority*

'I found the work to be a refreshing change from the run of the mill academic and sterile management books.... I was particularly taken with the concepts that make for good leadership that run through the book and especially the simple and uncluttered human understanding that can separate ordinary leaders from the great ones.... I very much enjoyed reading *Timeless Management*.'
John Conlon, *Chairman, Chorion plc*

'Too often books on management practice are utterly predictable – the same old concepts and the same old jargon. *Timeless Management* breaks the mould. This is an imaginative attempt to deal with the real life problems of management. The book has one extra virtue: Alan Coppin and John Barratt care about the workers. The employees are not regarded as some disposable asset or even as an inconvenient necessity. They are part of the business and their welfare is what makes the business thrive. *Timeless Management* is a thought-provoking manual of good practice.'
John Edmonds, *General Secretary, General Municipal and Boilermakers Union*

'This is an excellent management primer that cuts through the faddism of so many management theories, books and practices.... Moreover, there is a fine case study from the present day in which the authors put their theories into action ... it is as relevant to the rookie reader as it is the experienced professional. No reader can fail to draw some inspiration from its contents.'
Rob Cameron, *Chairman, Flag Communications*

'This book is a strong reminder that common sense was invented a long time ago.'
Paul Baines, *Managing Director, Hawkpoint*

'The best "how to" business book. Practical, user-friendly and illustrated with amusing anecdotes related to everyday modern business practice.'
Nicholas Hai, *CEO, Arrowcraft plc, Member of the Young Presidents Organisation*

'A very accessible and thought-provoking read for anyone in management or those interested in the motivations and behaviours of people.'
Mike Jolly CBE, *CEO, Penna Consulting plc*

'The book is a good read. I appreciated the people-orientated approach. I particularly valued the fact that you start by focusing on emotional make-up, values and integrity. I am sure the book will be a very successful management tool.'
William Weston, *CEO, The Royal Parks*

'This is an excellent guide for all managers, written in plain English and based upon common sense. The book sets a practical standard for us to aspire to.'
Sir Bruce MacPhail, *Managing Director, P&O; Chairman of the Council for School of Management Studies, Oxford University; Barclay Fellow of Templeton College, Oxford*

Timeless management

Alan Coppin and John Barratt

First published 2002 by
PALGRAVE MACMILLAN
Houndmills, Basingstoke, Hampshire RG21 6XS and
175 Fifth Avenue, New York, N.Y. 10010
Companies and representatives throughout the world

PALGRAVE MACMILLAN is the new global academic imprint of the Palgrave Macmillan division of St. Martin's Press LLC and of Palgrave Macmillan Ltd. Macmillan® is a registered trademark in the United States, United Kingdom and other countries. Palgrave is a registered trademark in the European Union and other countries.

ISBN 0-333-98080-8

This book is printed on paper suitable for recycling and made from fully managed and sustained forest sources.

A catalogue record for this book is available from the British Library.

A catalog record for this book is available from the Library of Congress.

Editing and origination by Curran Publishing Services, Norwich, Norfolk

10 9 8 7 6 5 4 3 2 1
11 10 09 08 07 06 05 04 03 02

Printed and bound in Great Britain by Creative Print & Design (Wales), Ebbw Vale

Contents

Contents

Preface

We hope this book appeals to (at least) two distinct reader groups: managers in organisations large and small (public, non-profit and private, profit seeking), who are all looking for business solutions; and enlightened individuals simply wanting to improve their own effectiveness. In our view the traits and most of the tools and techniques we outline are fully applicable to both groups. But perhaps it is particularly relevant for the public services who need to fully understand that it is not ministerial diktat or councillors' decrees or permanent secretaries' memos that get things done. Developing and trusting people is the only way to get improved results.

It is our intention for this book to be different. This is not in a vain attempt to increase sales. It actually is to mirror one of the guiding traits featured later in these pages. We hope the book is different in three ways:

- Principally, that it provides a different, easy to understand and hopefully interesting approach to increasing personal effectiveness at work and at home.
- Second, for those readers interested in the practical application of the timeless management traits, we hope to provide a live and ongoing case study. Apart from the Historic Royal Palaces case study in Part III of the book, we shall be providing regular updates on progress (or not), 'warts and all' reports via our Timeless Management website at www.timelessmanagement.com. These updates will be provided from June 2002 and each quarter thereafter.
- Last, we are actively seeking feedback from readers on the approach we have taken, our concept, our writing style and ways in which we could improve. Again this is in accordance with one of the important Timeless Management components: continuous improvement. Please contact us in writing at Historic Royal Palaces, Apartment 39, Hampton Court Palace, Surrey KT8 9AU, or via e-mail at www.timelessmanagement.com.

During the last year or so, we have been helped enormously in putting the book together by a large number of individuals, and we would like to thank them most sincerely for their time and assistance. We certainly do not want to repeat the mistake of the Duke of Wellington: as an old man, when asked by a friend what he would have done differently if he had his life over again, the Iron Duke replied, 'I should have given more praise.'

First and foremost we would like to thank our families to whom this book is dedicated with our love for their understanding, encouragement and support: Alan's family, his wife Gaynor and son Ed (who helped Alan to develop the Timeless Management concept for the book initially), and John's family, Jayne and James, and his mother and father, Jose and Bill, for making it possible in the first place!

Second, we are very grateful to the various teams of people who helped us from Historic Royal Palaces. Pam Heard and Anna Adil from Alan's office at Hampton Court have done an amazing job in typing up numerous iterations, in providing intelligent comments and retaining their sense of humour. Suzanne Groom and Anna Keay from the Palaces Curatorial department have contributed magnificently on the historical character illustrations and the context for their involvement in the Palaces. We thank Graham Josephs, the Personnel and Development Director, for his contributions and for overseeing the change programme. Sam Hearn, the internal auditor and a fervent closet historian, has provided a wealth of resource and background material. Rob Wood, IT manager, provided more up to date data on aspects of change. Annabelle Boyes and Peggy Sharkey initiated publisher contact and have given much needed retail and merchandising advice. Alyson Lawton, Trust and Company Secretary of Historic Royal Palaces, kindly reviewed Part III and checked it for accuracy. Field Marshal the Lord Inge, a Trustee, was extremely kind in commenting on the Timeless Management concept in its infancy and providing material on leadership.

We would pay special thanks and tribute to the Chairman of Historic Royal Palaces, the Earl of Airlie, who will complete his stint with the organisation in late 2002, and also to Lord Inge for, at least in part, inspiring this book by their everyday usage of most of the Timeless Management traits.

Our research task was made all the more easy by the excellent books on the market, and we are very grateful indeed to the authors listed in the bibliography section at the back of the book.

Stephen Rutt, our publisher from Palgrave, has guided us magnificently in what is a new world for us.

In addition, John would like to say a big 'thank you' to all the people he has worked with, both colleagues and clients, for helping to shape the thinking that is captured in this book. Special thanks are due to Paul Yorke for helping to launch his change management experiences, and for some valuable coaching early in his career, and to Angus MacLeod, and Peter McNair for helping him to understand how to be an effective consultant. David Williams and Derek Middleton: thanks to you for your support in helping him to think differently. Lastly, thanks to Fiona, Tania and the team in the Warehouse Café in the the House Shop in Bramhall for allowing him to write on their premises and for looking after him so well. If you are passing, they do a great toasted teacake!

So thank you to all the above for being there when the pages were blank.

As to the reader, please excuse us for spending so much time thanking people but as you will see, recognition is an important component of our book's theme.

Part I
Introduction

Work can provide the opportunity for spiritual and personal, as well as financial growth. If it doesn't we're wasting too much of our lives on it.

James Autry

1 Introduction

One of the many things we congratulate ourselves on as a species is our technical capability. Indeed, there is much to be proud of. Today we routinely perform things that would be 'miracles' to our great grandparents. We stretch our technology further and further in pursuit of new commercial opportunities. The speed of introduction of new ideas and new technology is breathtaking. Here are some simple examples.

- Apparently, if the automotive and aircraft industries developed at the same rate as semiconductors in the past 30 years, a Rolls-Royce would cost $2.75 and get 3 million miles to a gallon; and a Boeing 767 would cost $500 and circle the globe in 20 minutes on five gallons of gas.
- At the time of launch in 1981, IBM expected to sell approximately 240,000 PCs in five years. The year 2000 saw some 120–135 million PCs sold worldwide.
- The Intel 8086 chip used in early PCs had 29,000 transistors and could handle some 0.33 million instructions per second (mips). The Pentium 133MHz chip of the mid-1990s increased this to approximately 3.3 million transistors and 133 mips. The Pentium 4 chip, introduced in 2000, now has some 42 million transistors and can handle in excess of 1,500 mips.
- The cost of the basic specification IBM PC in 1981 was the equivalent of approx $5,500 in today's money. A PC today is well over 4,000 times more powerful in terms of pure processing power and typically costs 80 per cent less at under $1,200.

Science and technology are undoubtedly beneficial contributors to our world. They have enabled us to control our environment, fight disease, revolutionise communications, 'shrink the world', increase the rate and level of knowledge, provide mass entertainment and standards of living that historically were the preserve of a tiny elite.

3

At work, if correctly deployed, these advantages can be sources of productivity and competitive advantage.

However, technology can also be seductive. It can lead us to believe that it is the solution in itself, when usually it is no more than a tool. It draws us away from what is really important: the fact that results are always achieved by people. Organisations should always be about people and relationships. It is these human dimensions that make the difference between sustained success and obscurity. The same applies in our personal lives. People and relationships bring joy, learning and pleasure. They are also capable of bringing pain and frustration. At work and at home, it is easy to be drawn into valuing things more than people. Why do organisations commit huge investments in new information technology projects and spend a pittance on the involvement and training of the people who will use them? Why is it usually easier to seek investment for a new machine than to invest in the development of people and relationships? If many organisations proclaim 'people are our greatest asset', why do so many employees feel under-valued and disempowered? The Institute of Personnel and Development recently published results of a survey carried out by Gallup which suggested a staggering 63 per cent of UK workers are not engaged at work, 20 per cent are actively disengaged. This is estimated to cost the UK economy about £48 billion per annum. What a waste! How can organisations expect their people to give of their best and pledge their loyalty to the company when this is not reciprocated and at the first sign of an economic downturn they are fired? Short term thinking that doesn't even work in the short term – think of the impact on those who are left.

Our belief is that the underlying thinking is flawed. Technology is nothing more than an important tool. Improvement, innovation and knowledge reside in people. It is people who add value. They are the ones that make the difference. They are the only entities who can choose to serve customers and each other. They are the only true source of sustainable competitive advantage and meaning.

We are experiencing an ever-increasing gap. While our technology marches on apace, our thinking regarding organisations and people is rooted around the early years of the twentieth century. Over a number of decades we have developed a traditional way of thinking about management. Overall, this approach has been based on a few people having all the information and making all the decisions, and the workers being told what to do. This was born out of the move to mass production techniques. It is thinking that appears to value mechanistic approaches above people.

Deeper than this, and of more importance to this book, is the nature of our behavioural responses. The work done by evolutionary psychologists suggests that our emotional development is still anchored in our 'cave man' past. For almost 200,000 years humans lived in small groups as hunter-gatherers. In a world that was full of threats to life our instincts were key to survival. Our emotional responses to things saved lives. Then, about 7,000 years ago, agriculture developed, shaping a different kind of society where the vast majority of people lived on the land. The conditions of human life were dramatically transformed with the Industrial Revolution. Industry and commerce gave rise to an urban economy. The harnessing of machine power and technology rapidly accelerated and shifted the way we organise and live. In just over 200 years, a blink of an eye in evolutionary terms, we have experienced dramatic shifts in how we live our lives. Evolutionary psychologists point out that our brains are still 'hardwired' for our instinctive hunter-gatherer lifestyle. We just have not had enough time to evolve the genetic traits that are aligned to our current environment.

All humans have four basic needs:

- the need to feel comfortable
- the need to be understood
- the need to feel welcome/belong
- the need to feel important.

The key message here is straightforward. While the world has changed enormously, people haven't. While we pride ourselves on our capacity for rational thought, we are still predominantly emotional creatures. Our emotions override reason. How else can we explain fearing the new, leaping to assumptions and first impressions, forming cliques and showing suspicion of 'outsiders', following the crowd and being drawn into collective moaning?

Many of these behaviours are unhelpful and self-defeating in today's world. But they still persist. Here is the key. If our emotional make-up has been slow to evolve and change, then the qualities for effective management should also be timeless! By working to help satisfy the 'four basic needs' we can create a climate where people choose to be productive. An individual's commitment to a relationship, to a goal, a team or organisation is a voluntary activity. All we can do is create the kind of environment that makes it easy for people to volunteer. All else is coercion and control, and history is littered with examples of what happens inevitably when people are tired of being repressed. They rebel. Passively or aggressively, they seek to re-establish their 'four basic needs'.

Our aim in this publication is to spread our views and to understand and encourage people to value each other more; to share our experiences of how work and life can be more rewarding and more successful if we change our thinking and our behaviour. Margaret Young set out her interpretation of this idea when she wrote, 'Often people attempt to live their lives backwards; they try to have more things, or more money, in order to do more of what they want, so they will be happier. The way it actually works is in reverse. You must first be who you really are, then do what you need to do, in order to have what you want.'

This is the fundamental challenge. There is a huge gap between knowing and doing. Real results come from what we do – the application of what we know. If we are to change our behaviour than we must first change our thinking. To get the most value from this book we invite you to challenge your own thinking and your current behaviour. For the corporate reader, we hope the book and the implementation of the traits provide a framework for a plan for success, which is another way of describing a strategic plan. Most of the qualities we have identified can be learnt, and we hope to commence or refine the learning process in this book. In this connection we have included at the end of each chapter a tool box of practical actions and techniques to increase your effectiveness and thereby the effectiveness of your organisation.

We suggest that the rewards from this approach, corporate and personal, are significant. New (2001) research funded by the Economic and Social Research Council's Future of Work programme confirms that companies which value their employees and implement proper human resource practices (such as leadership development and training) are likely to be rewarded by enhanced financial performance (defined by profit per employee). In the twenty-first century the key battle will be the war for employing and keeping the best people. In the knowledge age it is the only competitive differentiator. Whether they like it or not, if organisations want to be successful they will have to develop an obsession for people. This is at the core of the concept of Timeless Management.

Summary

- Results are always achieved by people.
- While the world has changed enormously, people haven't.
- If our emotional make-up has changed little in 200,000 years, neither have the qualities for effective management. It is about creating an environment for ourselves and others that allows us to fulfil our 'four basic needs'.
- Real results come from what we do, the application of what we know. If we are to change our behaviour then we must first change our thinking.
- We judge ourselves by our intentions. We judge others by their actions. (It follows therefore that others judge us not by our words but by our actions.)

To get the most value from this book we invite you to challenge your own thinking and your current behaviour. Knowing is not the same as doing.

The Timeless Management concept

What lies behind us and what lies before us are tiny matters compared to what lies within us.

R. W. Emerson

Our invitation to Timeless Management is centred around five core qualities that set apart the mundane from the extraordinary, the plodder from the stellar performer: character; audacity; focus; clarity; mutuality. Each quality has a number of subsets. These traits are as applicable to individuals seeking to increase their personal effectiveness as they are to the corporate achiever. We have chosen to position this book on the management bookshelf, but we believe it would be equally valuable to anybody who just wants to achieve. After all, 'management' is not that complicated, it is only getting things done through people.

When undertaken on their own, the five characteristics undoubtedly add some value. But when applied together they are extremely powerful. As you will see these qualities overlap and, indeed, support each other. In this change driven, hi-tech boundary-less world, properly applied, they can be a major differentiator from the competition (whatever form that may take) and a great enabler.

Yet none of the traits have been recently invented. You don't need to have attended a business school and been awarded an MBA to discover or master the traits. There is nothing whatsoever complicated about them, in fact they are all founded on – basic common sense! Common sense underpins the whole Timeless Management concept. It is therefore important to define it. Not only is it the natural capacity for seeing things as they are (without illusion or any bias), it is also the ability to draw conclusions and to take appropriate action. All of those using Timeless Management featured in this book display common sense, but none more so than the Duke of Wellington. In his biography of Wellington, J. W. Fortescue wrote that the Duke's great gift was 'transcendent common sense, the rare power of seeing things as they are which signifies genius'. The Duke was also rather adept at translating perception into reality.

Moreover, our research indicates that the traits have been around and heavily practised for centuries. There is no need to invent funky new fads since well tried and effective ones that have stood the test of time are there, ready and waiting. They have been used consistently from the beginning of time and over the ages by thousands of historic figures, leaders and managers, but they have not previously been captured. What we have attempted to do is to draw together this wasted knowledge and create a 'new' management concept (but based on the 'old'), that of 'Timeless Management'.

In setting out this concept we aim, in our own small way, to at least partially challenge the assertion of Georg Hegel (the distinguished German idealist philosopher) when he wrote in his book *Philosophy of History* (1832): 'Peoples and governments never have learned anything from history, or acted on any principles deduced from it.' We also seek to disprove George Bernard Shaw's claim that 'We learn from experience, that men never learn anything from experience.'

It is some comfort that at least three of the late twentieth and early twenty-first centuries' most influential management and political leaders have also seen the benefit of learning from historical figures. Jack Welch, the legendary CEO of General Electric, has used the thinking of Prussian General Helmut von Moltke in forming his own views on strategy. Peter Drucker one of the twentieth century's most highly regarded management thinkers, drew wisdom from a number of historic sources, but particular favourites were from the nineteenth century literary world, novelists Jane Austen and Anthony Trollope.

Time magazine's 2001 Person of the Year, Rudy Giuliani, Mayor of New York City, is also a history man. He provides an example of learning from the past in an extreme crisis situation. If the approach is relevant in such circumstances, it is clearly adaptable to more mundane problems managers face in their everyday lives. At the end of his first punishing 16-hour stint immediately after the terrorist attacks, he returned to his bed. He didn't sleep. Instead, while watching the horrific scenes of the plane crashes being played time and again on television, he reached for a book on Winston Churchill, a long-time hero. He needed a historic figure to steer him through the mammoth task to come. Interestingly, he didn't consult the New York City disaster manual or seek words of wisdom from today's crisis management gurus. He looked to the past and chose Winston Churchill for his inspiration, as someone who himself inspired the people of Britain through the Second World War and, of more interest to Mayor Giuliani, the people of London through the blitz. Mr Giuliani figured that the same type of leadership qualities would be required of him, the example of Churchill and the people of London showed it could be done, and this provided some comfort in this dark hour.

He honed in on Churchill's words: 'I have nothing to offer but blood, toil, tears and sweat.' In the following three and a half months he was to live those words. In true Churchillian manner, when interviewed on television with his image being transmitted globally, his words were at the same time reassuring and defiant: 'Tomorrow New York is going to be here and we're going to rebuild and we're going to be stronger than before.' He continued, 'I want the people of New York to be an example to the rest of the country, and the rest of the world, that terrorism can't stop us.'

By his words and actions, the Mayor helped make Americans believe that losing to terrorists was just not an option. In a USA-wide *Time*/CNN poll conducted on 19/20 December 2001, 90 per cent believed New Yorkers' response to the 11 September attacks helped rally the rest of the USA, and an equally staggering 94 per cent said the Mayor had done a very good/good job in responding to the terrorist attacks on the World Trade Centre.

Of course, not all historic figures display positive traits all of the time. Even present day heroes like Mayor Giuliani didn't do this.

Indeed, some historic leaders are actually rather notorious for their negative characteristics: Henry VIII, for example, does not rapidly spring to mind as an enlightened management thinker or people person. Nevertheless, we do not consider that this Tudor monarch and others like him negate our core belief: that highly effective management techniques and concepts are timeless and simple to understand.

Moreover, although our sample of principal figures from history has been limited to England, we believe that the same traits are discernible in historical and more modern characters from around the globe. Accordingly, we have sprinkled the text with quotations and examples from a wider database.

For us this has not been a purely theoretical exercise, because the Timeless Management concept is actually used in practice to run Historic Royal Palaces, a number of the most important heritage buildings on the planet, and a leading visitor attraction business. It is also a charity, a non profit organisation, which represents a growing sector in the new economic order of the West. We would argue that if these characteristics can be successfully applied to these centuries-old institutions which have built up their own traditions and cultures, then they can be applied anywhere!

In this book we have chosen ten major historical figures, all connected with Historic Royal Palaces in some way, each one illustrating a particular Timeless trait and therefore qualifying as a historic manager of his or her time. That is not to say that these figures are paragons of virtue, people who would inhabit Sir Thomas More's Utopia! Far from it, they are all human. But they each illustrate at least one Timeless trait. It is, perhaps, bizarre to visualise Oliver Cromwell lecturing at the London Business School on the importance of 'audacity', but that is the essence of our idea. In the book we have also tried to set the trait in the context of the personality and contribution of the historic figure.

In Part II we set out the five traits and provide examples of their use by our historic figures. There is a summary section for each trait, together with a toolbox of techniques for you to use as a means of increasing effectiveness.

In Part III we provide a modern example of the traits and Timeless Management philosophy in use by way of a case study in the Historic Royal Palaces organisation of today, hopefully showing that we practise what we preach. We bring this right up to date by outlining how the Timeless Management approach shaped the palaces' response to the indirect impact of the 11 September 2001 terrorist attack on our business. We also show how we intend to keep this case study alive for readers of Timeless Management through regular updates on the www.timelessmanagement.com web site. But more of this later ... you have to read the book first!

Part II
The key timeless traits

There is no one who cannot vastly improve their powers of leadership by a little thought and practice.

Field Marshal Slim (1891–1970)

If you are planning for one year, plant rice. If you are planning for ten years, plant trees. If you are planning for 100 years, plant people.

Chinese proverb

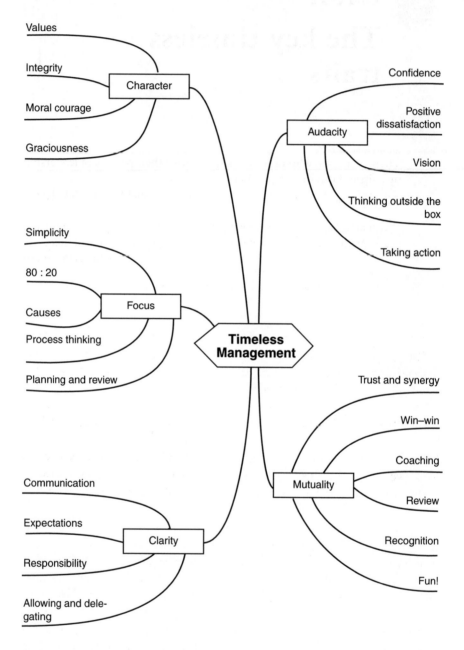

Values

Integrity

Character

Moral courage

Graciousness

Confidence

Positive
dissatisfaction

Audacity

Vision

Thinking outside the
box

Taking action

Simplicity

80 : 20

Focus

Causes

Process thinking

Planning and review

Timeless
Management

Trust and synergy

Win–win

Coaching

Mutuality

Review

Recognition

Fun!

Communication

Expectations

Clarity

Responsibility

Allowing and dele-
gating

Figure 2.1 The Timeless Management five traits model

2 Character

Character is what you are in the dark.
> D. L. Moody (1837–1899)

We make a living by what we do, we make a life by who we are.

In a world obsessed with doing, we believe the first and critical step is 'being'.

If you cannot manage yourself, how can you expect to lead others?

If you are unclear on what you stand for, why should anyone choose to follow you?

If you have no clear 'inner compass' of core beliefs, how can you prioritise and make valid choices and decisions?

Our behaviour indicates our character. It is the outward expression of what we hold to be important. We are who we choose to be. Theodore Roosevelt, 26th President of the United States, chose to be a moral leader. His contemporary, writer Mark Twain, described the President's behaviour as 'joyous ebullitions of excited sincerity'. Twain believed this behaviour in large measure accounted for him being 'the most popular human being that has ever existed in the United States'. The American novelist Henry James wrote of Roosevelt, 'a really extraordinary creature for native intensity, veracity and bonhomie'. At least for these two literary figures, Roosevelt was who he chose to be.

We are emotional creatures and our instincts draw us toward those whom we trust and guide us away from those whom we suspect. If we hope for others to respect us, there has to be something of substance to respect. By thinking about what is really important to us, and how we want to 'be' in our lives, we can exercise control over our instinctive 'automatic' selves.

Thoughts involuntarily coming from our memory can make us look at new situations through a filter of past experience. We are at risk of making many decisions as past-based machines. This is good and bad. It protects us from making the same mistake again, but limits our ability to imagine radically new possibilities for ourselves. It can make us resistant to change if we 'automatically' perceive the new as a threat. 'Following the herd' behaviour is largely an automatic response. Habits are 'automatic' memory-based decisions. However, we can escape from the history of the past by making conscious choices about what is really important to us in how we want to 'be'.

This requires us to accept responsibility for our lives, to avoid blaming others or circumstances and to take charge of our choices. We are where we are in our lives due to the choices that we have made. If we are unhappy with where we are, maybe it is time to make some new choices.

Ultimately, the only things we can control are our choices. We cannot control the outcomes of these choices, there are too many variables at work. We may choose to get the early train to increase the odds of arriving on time. But we cannot guarantee that we will. We are not in a position to control events. The best we can ever do is influence things. But we have the power to choose.

We can choose our attitude. Each morning we can choose to be happy or moody. Either attitude probably takes the same amount of energy. In every situation we can choose how to react to it. If things don't go as well as we hoped we can choose to moan and play the victim, or we can choose to accept responsibility for our choice, learn from it, and move on.

When people choose to moan and be negative, we can choose to join in or choose to seek the positive. If we need a simple example we need look no further than the English and their obsession with the weather. Wherever a group of people gather and talk about the weather there is a high probability that someone will moan about it. It will either be too wet (very often!), too hot or too 'something'. As soon as this starts, the conversation takes a slide as all involved feel compelled to join in on how bad things are:

Nothing to do but work!
Nothing! alas, alack!
Nowhere to go but out!
Nowhere to come but back!

We can choose the opposite if we wish.

Much has been written about 'leadership'. Relatively little attention has been given to 'followership'. People choose their leaders. You cannot make someone respect an individual because of their formal status or position. In 1654 Oliver Cromwell did not confuse the cheering of a crowd with respect for him and remarked, 'The people would be just as noisy if they were going to see me hanged.' People choose to give their respect to other individuals. To do so, they need to perceive something worthy of respect. This is the role of character. This is what Lord Rosebery meant when he said of William Pitt the Elder, 'It is not merely the thing that is said, but the man who says it that counts, the character which breathes through the sentences.'

It is important to make a distinction here. We are not referring to 'charisma', or the cult of the individual. Such traits may be highly beneficial, but unless they are genuine personality characteristics they are unlikely to develop respect. Our experience is that the opposite is likely. Most people will spot a charlatan, especially over the long term.

We define 'character' as clarity about what you stand for as an individual and the consistent expression of these beliefs in your behaviour. People judge us, rightly or wrongly, on what we do not what we say.

In selecting men for his New Model Army Oliver Cromwell went for character and values over birth and patronage. His selection criteria included men:

- who had the fear of God in them
- who made some conscience of what they did
- that know what they fight for
- and live what they know.

He promoted by character and merit. This army became a very powerful fighting force.

We believe there are four key components of character: our values, our integrity, moral courage and graciousness.

Values

> You must become the change you want to see in the world.
> Mahatma Gandhi (1869–1948)

Our values are the key beliefs that we hold to be guiding lights. They define how we choose to live our lives. If we have no clarity on our values, what criteria do we use to decide on right or wrong? Our core beliefs, the principles we hold to be of value, condition our behaviour.

As we deal with people all we can see is their behaviour, verbal and non-verbal, and that is all they can see of us. Our behaviour is what develops or destroys respect from other people.

The next deeper layer is attitude. The *Webster's Dictionary* definition of 'attitude' is 'mental position with regard to a fact or state': in other words, all the assumptions we make about life and people.

The deepest layer is that of beliefs and values. These are our deeply held beliefs about life: what we have learned to value. These condition our attitudes, that is, our assumptions about life and people.

Behaviour can be described as everything we say and do and how we say and do it. Our behaviour has a direct impact on the results we get in our lives. It is the only way other people have to make decisions about who we are as individuals, and how they feel about us.

At any point in our lives some of our behaviour will be helping us achieve the things that we value. Some of it will not. It will be holding us back. It will be 'self-defeating behaviour'. Nothing changes unless behaviour changes. If we continue to do what we have always done we will continue to get what we have always got.

Many people assume that behaviour 'just happens'. This is not the case. Everything we say and do starts as a thought. All behaviour starts from our thinking.

By 'watching ourselves' we can spot unhelpful 'self-defeating' behaviours. We can then change our thinking to break the old habit and replace it with new thinking that will lead to more helpful behaviour. This can be thought of as an 'onion ring'.

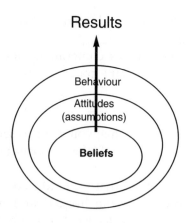

Figure 2.2

The results we get in our life are a product of our behaviour. Our behaviour is shaped by our attitudes. Our attitudes are driven by our beliefs. If we want a change in the results we experience, we must start with a shift in thinking. This will drive different, more helpful behaviour.

This also links strongly with commitment. We show our true commitment through our behaviour. If we 'talk a good game' about the importance of, say, trust, but keep gossiping, our behaviour shows that we are not really committed to trust. Our values shape our assumptions and attitudes, which then drive our behaviour. When our behaviour is in tune with our values we experience integrity.

In many situations we may decide we do not have freedom of choice, and behave in order to get acceptance from, or avoid confrontation with, the people we interact with. When this behaviour is not in line with our internal values this can cause inner conflict and feelings like annoyance, confusion, and low self-esteem. In extreme cases this inner conflict can lead to serious stress. A key aspect of managing yourself and others is to develop capability to manage this tension between being free to choose behaviour in line with your values and having to adopt behaviour to survive in the environment you are in.

Let us explore this connection between beliefs and behaviour through an example. Imagine manager number one, someone who believes that, in general, people are lazy, cannot be trusted and are not reliable. What are the likely associated attitudes/assumptions? Probably something along the lines of, 'I need to check everything and keep a tight rein on things.' What behaviour is this likely to lead to? We would suggest very close supervision and control, and perhaps even coercion or threatening behaviour in order to obtain adequate effort toward the achievement of organisational objectives.

Now let us consider another manager, number two, someone who believes that, in general, people have a need to achieve, are trustworthy and dependable, and are willing to take responsibility for things that interest and challenge them. This would lead to trust-based behaviour and a more participatory style of management.

Now let us put the two scenarios together. What is likely to happen if people like manager number two find themselves working in an organisation with a very strong 'command and control' culture? The chances are that they will take one of two routes. They will stick to their values regarding how they believe they should manage other people. By pursuing this they risk conflict and criticism from their bosses and the rest of the 'system'. Over time this could become corrosive and draining. The second route is to adapt their behaviour to the 'command and control' environment they are in. This could easily undermine their self-esteem and commitment, as they feel they are 'living a lie' each and every day at work. This also produces an unhealthy inner stress. In both scenarios the individual suffers and the organisation loses productivity.

Values have a hard commercial edge, especially in an economic climate where there is a 'war' for talent. Commitment and excellence are voluntary activities. People choose to offer and strive for them. They are only likely to make this choice and offer if they feel aligned with the aims and values of the organisation. It still surprises us how many recruitment and selection decisions are made without assessing whether there is an appropriate fit between the values of the organisation and the values of the individual. Organisations are often guilty of assessing suitability solely on technical skill and experience. Individuals often spend too much time thinking about 'the package' and too little on choosing an environment (and a boss) that is aligned to their personal values.

A clear values framework should be at the heart of our decision making. Without such a clear framework we run the risk of being 'at the mercy of the winds', inconsistent, indecisive and even apathetic. Decisions made on values increase your confidence and self-esteem. They sharpen your sense of self.

Integrity

> Integrity without knowledge is weak and useless, and knowledge without integrity is dangerous and dreadful.
>
> Samuel Johnson, 1759

'Integrity' is derived from the root word 'integer', meaning 'oneness or wholeness'. We are more likely to experience integrity when our choices and behaviour are in line with our values.

We build integrity when we are consistent in what we think, say and do. When there is inconsistency between what we think and say and do, it causes inner conflict and reduces our self-esteem and self-confidence. We feel out of tune with ourselves and may experience the corrosive feelings of guilt.

Whenever other people experience the inconsistency between what we say and what we do, it undermines their feelings of trust in us. Clearly, the Duke of Wellington experienced this feeling: 'They [cabinet ministers] agree to what I say in the morning, and then in the evening they start up with some crotchet which deranges the whole plan.' Trust can be hard to win and easy to lose.

The simple but challenging task of keeping our agreements – actually doing what we say we are going to do – builds our self-esteem and increases other people's trust in us. However, to achieve this requires that we fully embrace honesty. Honesty is a key building block of integrity. If others perceive us to be dishonest it puts distance between us. If we break our promises we appear dishonest. If team members view their manager as dishonest they will always hear and see everything through a filter of suspicion. They are unlikely to freely choose to commit their enthusiasm and support. It makes it more difficult for people to self-motivate.

Honesty is always a choice that is available to us, but it requires courage and confidence. It involves risk because it may bring disapproval or confrontation with other people. Often it is easier to agree with others or to say nothing. Sometimes this is appropriate: making a stand on every trivial issue can easily lead to being viewed as obstructive and pedantic. It could be argued that Oliver Cromwell took the concept of honesty a little too far when he warned his portrait painter, 'Mr Lely, I desire you would use all your skill to paint my true picture like me, and not flatter me at all; but remark all these roughnesses, pimples, warts and everything as you see me, otherwise I will never pay a farthing for it.' However, not being honest about how we feel on important issues, especially those that conflict with one of our values, causes internal tension. We do not feel true to ourselves and our self-esteem diminishes as a consequence.

Being honest with ourselves and with others builds integrity. Integrity builds self-esteem and self-confidence and develops trust. Trust reduces suspicion and creates an environment where people find it easier to offer commitment and take responsibility. Oliver Cromwell understood this when in 1642 he wrote in a letter to Robert Barnard, 'Subtlety may deceive you, integrity never will.' A more modern authority, Peter Drucker, set out his views on the importance of integrity in his legendary book *The Practice of Management*, when he wrote 'No matter what a man's general education or his adult education for management, what will be decisive above all, in the past, is neither education nor skill; it is integrity of character.' We agree with Professor Drucker: honesty and integrity are powerful and central aspects of Timeless Management. We should apply them to managing ourselves first, so we are fit to lead others.

Moral courage

> I am convinced from studying great military and other leaders and from the people for whom I have worked that moral courage is a higher and greater virtue than physical courage. It is a fundamental quality – without it other qualities are unlikely to be exercised.
>
> Field Marshal the Lord Inge, Deputy Chairman, Historic Royal Palaces, 2000

In order to be honest with ourselves and others, to develop and sustain integrity, we need moral courage. Here we are making the distinction between two types of courage. The courage that is most usually referred to is 'physical' courage, the willingness to risk injury or even death. What we are referring to with 'moral courage' is having the courage of your convictions. In other words, being clear on your values is of little worth if you are not courageous enough to live by them.

Remember, we live in integrity, and feel 'whole' when our actions are aligned with our values – what we believe to be right. This helps us to feel more fulfilled as individuals and builds trust and commitment with others. However, it may take great courage to 'stand out from the herd'. To speak the truth may carry risk to relationships. But if that truth is fundamental to the relationship itself, we need the courage to take the risk.

This can be observed in organisations. Managers may shield their team members from the harsh realities of business life for fear that they will be demotivated by the bad news. They may also fear the question, 'So what's going to be done about it?' because they do not have an answer. If people are unaware of the harsh reality, how can they take any responsibility for improving the situation? If they are ignorant of the need, why should they change their behaviour or make sacrifices in order to resolve the problem? If we treat them like children they are likely to respond like children. When it later comes to light that the manager(s) did know the harsh realities but did not communicate them, trust and confidence in the relationship is corroded.

Moral courage is also a state of mind. It is the engine room of character. Without it the other qualities will not come into play. It is the self-discipline and determination to do what is right, to be true to yourself and others by living your values. It is also the willpower to make and take the important and difficult decisions in your job and your life. Making the decision is the first and important step and will test your moral courage. The second step is actioning it: making sure that it takes place and takes root. This can require significant courage when the decision is in the face of 'conventional wisdom', or when change is needed if improvement is to be attained.

> Tender handed stroke a nettle,
> And it stings you for your pains,
> Grasp it like a man of mettle,
> And it soft as silk remains.
>   Aaron Hill, 1794

Graciousness

> The foundation of all excellent manners is majesty ... and is properly a beauty or comeliness in countenance, language and gesture apt to dignity and fitting to time, place and company: which, like as the sun does his beams, so does it cast on the beholders and heroes a pleasant and terrible reverence.
>   Sir Thomas Elyot (1490–1546)

> Merit is not enough unless supported by grace.
>   Gracian, 1647

> Every action done in company ought to be with some sign of respect to those who are present.
>   George Washington (1732–1799)

Ever really wanted to meet someone because you admired them, or what they stood for? Ever met them and felt really disappointed because they were so full of their own importance?

Ever known or worked with someone who is arrogant? How about someone who wants everyone to know how good they are, or how much money they have?

What about those people who seem determined to show you that they are better than you, who put some distance between you?

How do you feel towards them?

If the only way we can feel good about ourselves is by proving that we are better than others, we are living from insecurity. We are not being true to ourselves, and so we seem empty and pretentious to others.

Eisenhower, the great US general (Supreme Commander for the 1944 invasion of the continental mainland) and US President summed this up when he wrote:

> A sense of humility is a quality I have observed in every leader whom I have deeply admired. I have seen Winston Churchill with humble tears of gratitude on his cheeks as he thanked people for their help to Britain and the allied cause.
>
> My own conviction is that every leader should have enough humility to accept, publicly, the responsibility for the mistakes of the subordinates he has himself selected and, likewise, to give them credit, publicly, for their triumphs. I am aware that some popular theories of leadership hold that the top man must always keep his 'image' bright and shining. I believe, however, that in the long run fairness and honesty, and a generous attitude towards subordinates and associates, pay off.

If we are trying to prove that we are better than others, it suggests that we believe we are better than them. So how does that make them feel?

Ego-driven behaviour – arrogance, piety, 'one-upmanship', aggression, sarcasm, (to mention but a few) – causes distance and reduces trust and commitment in relationships. If we are clear on our values and live by them we have a strong sense of our own integrity and worth. We do not need to make others feel bad in order for us to feel good.

Graciousness is how we behave. It involves treating others with respect, and by living by example not by proclamation. George Washington believed from an early age that civility and success went hand in hand. While still in his teens he prepared a list of behavioural guidelines entitled *122 Rules for Civility and Decent Behaviour in Company and Conversation*. These included, 'Speak not evil of the absent for it is unjust; speak not injurious words, neither lie in jest or earnest and scoff at none although they give occasion; use no reproachful language against anyone; neither curse or revile.'

It might also involve use of a really underrated form of compensation: 'Thanks.'

Graciousness is a standard of excellence, it is a gift of yourself to others, the donation of your attention, your interest, your listening and your caring. It builds trust and fortifies relationships. A modern day example of this type of approach in business was given proudly by Bob Galvin, speaking of his father who was founder of the Motorola Organisation: 'Dad once looked down an assembly line of women employees and thought, "These are all like my own Mum – they have kids, homes to take care of, people who need them." It motivated him to work hard to give them a better life because he saw his Mum in all of them. That's how it all begins – with fundamental respect.'

The experience of Motorola showed that deep respect for individuals did not jar with economic performance. In fact quite the reverse: Peter Drucker argues that 'when graciousness declines, the end is near'. It is too early at the time of writing this book to determine that arrogance and a lack of graciousness was the key reason for the demise of Enron, the biggest corporate collapse in the history of the world. But it is likely to have been a contributory factor in an organisation whose leaders had the breathtaking arrogance in their advertisements to liken themselves to (rather than learn from) great figures such as Mahatma Gandhi and Martin Luther King. Moreover, the antithesis of graciousness – arrogance and bullying – in the workplace can cause real and lasting damage to organisations and people. Such damage can go beyond the obvious drop in morale and productivity: poor health can result for the individual.

On the positive side, companies that exhibit graciousness and respect for individuals are likely to be more sought after in the twenty-first century battle to attract and retain talent. The knock-on benefits can include higher morale from staff who feel highly valued and from belonging to a company with high standards. Enhanced team spirit is another by-product. This leads to greater productivity.

All of this starts with our behaviour, which is the manifestation of our character. How do others see us? How do we want to be seen and remembered? Sometimes we may forget that we are subject to the same standards we expect of others, and that being ungracious could be to our personal detriment, as well as to the disadvantage of the organisation.

Character: key points

- Being responsible for your own choices, actions and consequences is fundamental to building character.
- Our behaviour indicates our character. It is the outward expression of what we hold to be important.
- By exercising choice we can modify our 'automatic' responses to situations and people.
- We can choose who we want to be.
- We can choose how we react to any situation.
- In order to choose we need clarity on what we stand for, what is important to us. We describe these things as values.
- Our values act as an internal compass, helping us choose the appropriate direction, and giving a yardstick for our decisions.
- When our choices are aligned with our values we are acting in integrity. This helps us to feel 'whole'.
- In order to act in integrity, we need moral courage to be honest with ourselves and with others.
- Integrity builds self-esteem and self-confidence and develops trust.
- Trust reduces suspicion and creates an environment where people find it easier to offer commitment and take responsibility.
- Graciousness is a gift of yourself to others, the donation of your attention, your interest, your listening and your caring. It builds trust and fortifies relationships.
- Honesty, graciousness and integrity are powerful aspects of Timeless Management. We should apply them to managing ourselves first, so we are fit to lead others.

Toolbox

There are no quick fixes for building character, it is a lifelong exercise. Still, every journey needs to start with the first step, so choose some quiet time for yourself, fix your favourite drink and have a think about the following questions.

In case you're wondering: no, there is no worked example, it is something we need to work out for ourselves. The questions are simple but challenging; they will take time to answer. It is worth revisiting them over several different sessions. We suggest you set out the following questions on a blank sheet of paper and then spend some time answering them.

A What is your purpose in life?

Unless we consciously decide what is important in our lives we are at risk of operating 'automatically' based on past experiences or what the media encourage us to be.

A.1   Who are the people who really matter to you in your life?
A.2   What do you want people to say about you after they have met you?
A.3   At the end of your days what do you want to be remembered for?

My purpose is to …

B What is your purpose as a leader?

B.1   What do you want your team members to be saying about you?
B.2   What do you want your customers to be saying about you?
B.3   What do you want your boss to be saying about you?
B.4   What do you want your suppliers to be saying about you?

My purpose as a leader is to …

C Deducing the values that support your purpose

Again we propose you set out the following questions to answer on a blank sheet of paper. Leave plenty of space between questions for your answers. Our values should be deduced from our purpose: in other words, ask yourself, 'What are the bedrock beliefs I need to hold and practise if I am to fulfil my purpose?' Look through your answers to the previous questions. What trends are there? What are the underpinning values, the things that you need to 'live' in order to achieve your purpose? (Examples might be 'relationships', 'commitment' and 'integrity'.)

- *Value*
  Why?
- *Value*
  Why?

27

- *Value*
  Why?
- *Value*
  Why?
- *Value*
  Why?
- *Value*
  Why?
- *Value*
  Why?
- *Value*
  Why?

Timeless Management historical illustrations

Timeless Manager 1: Sir Thomas More – character

Sir Thomas More (1478–1535), also St Thomas More (feast day 22 June). He studied at Oxford University, and became a lawyer. He spent a number of years in a Carthusian monastery but did not take holy orders. For Henry VIII he became Master of Requests, Treasurer of the Exchequer, Chancellor of the Duchy of Lancaster and Lord Chancellor.

Connections with Historic Royal Palaces

In his days of favour, Thomas More was often at Hampton Court and York Place (later called Whitehall Palace), both when they were still Cardinal Wolsey's houses and after they had been appropriated by Henry VIII. He witnessed Wolsey's expansion of both buildings, and even remarked to the Cardinal at York Place, 'I like this gallery of yours, my Lord, much better than your gallery at Hampton Court.' After Wolsey's fall, it was in the gallery at Hampton Court that Henry VIII broached with More the question of his divorce, an occasion described by More himself: 'Suddenly His Highness, walking in the gallery, brake with me of his great matter...'.

More's inability to sanction the break with the Church of Rome, which Henry VIII saw as the only way to secure his divorce, brought him eventually to the Tower, accused of treason. Here More spent the last months of his life, incarcerated in a cell, eventually deprived of his writing materials, and from here he was led to his execution on Tower Hill on 6 July 1535.

Historical illustration

Thomas More appeared to be more than normally interested in the derrière. He quite often used the swear words 'arse' and 'shit', particularly in his religious war of words with Martin Luther, the German Protestant.

During his period as Lord Chancellor, More was responsible for, and had no compunction about, the burning of heretics.

In a man of great learning and intelligence and one who abhorred violence these two human failings appear incongruous and incomprehensible in twenty-first century terms. The burnings may be a little easier to explain when it is understood that not only were public executions commonplace at this time, but that as a boy More himself passed an execution site twice each day on his way to and from school. There were no 'U' certificates in the 1480s; children witnessed all, and therefore More was in line with contemporary thinking in his support for what were for us barbaric practices. His fascination for the anal cannot be so easily explained, although may derive from beatings he received at his strict school, St Anthony's. But despite his use of colourful expletives and his backing of the use of the stake, More was a man of great character, integrity and moral courage. Quite simply, in the final analysis, he was prepared to die for his beliefs. For this he was canonised in 1935.

He was named after another saint, Thomas Becket. Curiously Becket had been born only a stone's throw from Mill Street where More was born on 7 February 1478. His values were imbued at an early age, when virtues such as piety and honesty were more important than material wealth or high office.

More was to serve for a period in the household of the Archbishop of Canterbury and Lord Chancellor, John Morton, a man also considered at the time to be a man of integrity. This appointment precluded More from going to Eton but it was considered a great honour and as it turned out gave him an early insight into his later career in royal politics.

It was Morton who supported More's application to Canterbury College, Oxford, which he joined at age 14 (quite usual for the time). He did not stay to take his degree and, encouraged by his father, he left Oxford at 16 to join New Inn to take up a career in the law. This was the start of an extraordinary career in jurisprudence and administration which culminated in his appointment in 1529 to the highest office of all, Lord Chancellor.

More used two guiding principles throughout his life: common sense and belief in custom or habit (and not reinventing the wheel). He is famously described by his friend Erasmus as 'omnium horarum' – a man for all seasons. This means a man who is affable and has a sweet nature. When combined with his natural intelligence and generally pleasing personality, the application of these tenets perhaps explains More's astonishing performance in the corridors of power.

More lived during a time when most of the population was illiterate and when there was great respect for people who could read. In fact lay scholars could literally get away with murder – although as punishment for their first offence they would have their forehead branded with a letter 'M'!

Someone of More's scholarly standing must have been revered, particularly following release of his various publications including *Utopia*. In this book More describes an imaginary island representing the perfect society, an ingenious device to share idealistic values.

There are numerous examples in his life when More acted with honesty and integrity. While at Oxford he heard that some of the poorer scholars were being badly treated by certain shopkeepers who were over-charging them. He convinced the burgesses of Oxford that this was wrong and had the money returned to him. He duly repaid the scholars.

More was an esteemed adviser to King Henry VIII. On one occasion the King visited him at his home in Chelsea. While walking in the garden, the King showed his trust and affection of More by putting his arm around his shoulder. This was not appreciated at all by More – he at all times wanted to keep his distance and his integrity sound.

Another example of his high principle can be seen when, as Lord Chancellor, he became involved in a case involving his son-in-law who he found against. He is quoted as saying to William Roper, 'Were it my father stood on the one side and the devil on the other, his cause be good, the devil should have right.' Such resolution to do the right thing could, perhaps, only be expected from this pious man who as a youth and later under his splendid robes of office wore a hair shirt (made of itchy and uncomfortable haircloth) as a penance.

Throughout his career More was seen by his contemporaries as a man of the utmost honour and integrity. He had a reputation when he was a judge of making decisions fairly and fast. When presented with a rather petty domestic case, the alleged purloining of a poor woman's dog by his second wife, Alice More, he set up a simple test. He made the women stand apart and call the dog. The dog ran to the poor woman. Justice was doubly satisfied when the poor woman agreed to sell the dog to Alice.

A rather different level of praise was bestowed on More by the Duke of Norfolk when on More's appointment as Lord Chancellor of England he made a speech praising More's wisdom and virtue. Sadly, this view of More by the King was not to last (and in 1532 More resigned the Chancellorship).

Thomas More did not approve of Henry VIII's divorce from Catherine of Aragon, but the 'divorce' proceeded and early in 1533 Henry married a pregnant Anne Boleyn. It was in July of that year that the King was excommunicated by Pope Clement VII. The break with Rome was nigh. In March 1534 the Act of Succession was passed by Parliament. This Act stated not only that King Henry VIII's marriage to Anne Boleyn was lawful but also that his marriage to Catherine of Aragon was legally void. To More the aim of the Act was evident: to declare independence of the English Church from Rome. Menacingly, the Act stated that anyone attacking the marriage of the King to Anne would be guilty of treason. Furthermore, commissioners were sent throughout the kingdom requiring people to swear an oath supporting the Act.

More was summoned to Lambeth Palace on Monday, 13 April 1534 and asked to swear the oath: he refused on two occasions and was subsequently committed to the Tower of London. Following a number of interrogations in the Tower when More bravely and steadfastly maintained his position, he was taken to Westminster Hall for his famous trial. He was convicted of treason. Five days later he was taken to the scaffold on Tower Hill. And so Thomas More had the moral courage to stay true to his beliefs and to make the ultimate personal sacrifice.

Of course only in the rarest and most extreme of circumstances would such a sacrifice be even considered for ordinary mortals. But this does not negate the importance for us all to stay true to our beliefs. Perhaps a more relevant current-day version of paying a high price for our beliefs might be a decision to leave a job perhaps due to a conflict with our employer's values, with the economic and social consequences that flow from this. At another level it might simply involve having the moral courage to stand up and be counted, resisting something we believe to be wrong in a work or social setting.

Hopefully, what is provided by Sir Thomas More is the example: if he was prepared to pay the ultimate and unthinkable price, then perhaps it becomes a little easier for us to take decisive but obviously less drastic action in order to stay true to our principles.

Timeless Manager 2: George III – graciousness

King George III (1738–1820), King of Great Britain and Ireland (1760–1820), Elector (1760–1815) and King (from 1815) of Hanover, born in London.

Connection with Historic Royal Palaces

After his father's death in 1751, the young Prince George (soon to become George III) and his brother Frederick moved into the Dutch House at Kew, now known as Kew Palace. It continued to be one of George's favourite residences during his reign, and he and his wife Charlotte spent much time here. On several occasions in his later life, when suffering his periods of 'madness' (probably porphyria), the King was forcibly brought to Kew, to keep him away from public gaze.

In July 1818 two of George and Charlotte's children, William, Duke of Clarence (later William IV) and Edward, Duke of Kent (father of Queen Victoria), were married and a sumptuous double wedding breakfast was served for them that morning at Kew. Sadly, four months later George's beloved wife, Queen Charlotte, died at Kew Palace. Her body lay in state there before being transferred to Windsor for her funeral.

During his reign George III never considered living at either Kensington Palace or Hampton Court Palace because they brought back unhappy childhood memories. He particularly disliked Hampton Court. In 1770, when he was informed shortly after it started that a fire had broken out in the Palace, he reputedly said that he would not have been sorry if the whole place had been burnt down.

Historical illustration

> George the Third
> Ought never to have occurred
> One can only wonder
> At so grotesque a blunder.
>   Edmund Clerihew Bentley (1875–1956)

The rather sad rhyme above refers to one view of the longest-serving king: the period from 1810 when he became permanently deranged and medically unfit to rule when his son, later George IV, took over from him as Prince Regent. But it was very much based on a minority view. Despite heading the nation at the time of losing the American colonies and his subsequent madness caused by the physical disease, porphyria, George III was loved by the vast majority of his people.

The affection is evidenced throughout his reign but especially on his death when there was an outpouring of grief and the whole country, including the poor, went into mourning. Two quotes sum up this feeling. The first is from Mrs Arbuthnot, friend of the Duke of Wellington: 'And thus has sunk into an honoured grave the best man and the best king that ever adorned humanity.' Another quote from Sir Nathaniel Wroxall: 'Never, I believe, did any prince – not even Elizabeth, leave behind him a memory more cherished by his subjects.' So what generated such emotion?

Before 1810 when he became permanently deranged he had been a strong, hard-working and decisive monarch, and despite the loss of the American colonies, he ruled over what was undoubtedly at the time the most significant empire in the world. His popularity was enhanced by his support for the wars with France (following the French Revolution).

George was a cultured although not outstandingly intelligent monarch. He made major contributions to the development of knowledge through his collection of books which numbered 65,000 when they were given to the British Museum to start a British Library. He also funded and founded the Royal Academy of Arts and he was interested in science – a number of scientific instruments he collected are now on show in the Science Museum in London. He gave financial support to a large number of writers, artists, scientists and musicians. But this interest in the furtherance of knowledge could not of itself explain his popularity.

George III exhibited a number of 'gracious' qualities, including humility and empathy with his people and it is perhaps these that were readily recognised and prized by his people. During the bread shortages of the late eighteenth century he insisted that the Royal Household ate only brown bread, as the rest of the population was forced to do.

On another occasion, sitting alone in his library, he called the page in waiting to bring some coal for the fire. On arrival the page promptly rang the bell for the footman to carry out this task. It was the footman's job to perform such a task, despite the fact that he was advanced in years. Immediately, the King asked the page to show him where the coal was kept and he fetched it himself. On so doing he turned to the page and said, 'Never ask an old man to do what you are so much better able to do yourself.'

George III had an ability to relate to and empathise with ordinary people and showed he respected them by recognising them regardless of age. A local shopkeeper said that the King 'knew something of the character and affairs of most persons who lived under the shadow of the (Windsor) castle'. On one occasion the King was walking in Great Park, Windsor when he came across a boy. He asked the boy who he was and the boy replied, 'I be pig boy but I don't work. They don't want lads here. All this belongs to Georgy.' The King enquired who 'Georgy' was. The reply came, 'He is King and he lives at the castle, but he does no good to me.' The King ensured the boy was given a job on one of his farms.

On another occasion he was at one of his farms and spotting a woman working alone, he went to talk to her. He enquired where everyone had gone. She replied that they had gone to see the King but that she 'wouldn't give a pin to see him' and that they were fools because they would forfeit their wage for the day. She went on to say that she could not afford to join them as she had five children to support. He immediately gave her some money and said, 'You may tell your companions who are gone to see the King that the King came to see you.'

George was even concerned at the treatment of a woman, Margaret Nicholson, who had tried to kill him; 'Take care of the woman,' he said, 'do not hurt her, for she is mad.'

His handling of people of 'higher rank' was also done with a certain style. One example of this occurred at Queen's House, as Buckingham House, now Buckingham Palace, was then popularly known. Samuel Johnson, the lexicographer and writer, used to visit one of the four libraries George III had established in Queen's House. On hearing this the King asked the librarian to tell him when Johnson next visited. This he did, and the King followed the librarian to the room Johnson was reading in and surprised him while deep in a book. It is reported that 'his Majesty approached him and at once was courteously easy'. The two men spent some time discussing a range of topics from Oxbridge universities to a number of literary works. During the course of the conversation the King asked Johnson if he was currently writing anything. Johnson replied in the negative, adding that he thought he had 'told the world what he knew' and that he had fulfilled his role as a writer. The King elegantly replied, 'I should have thought so too, if you had not written so well.' Johnson was delighted with the compliment paid by George, and he later told the librarian, 'Sir, they may talk of the King as they will: but he is the finest gentleman I have ever seen ... his manners are those of as fine a gentleman as we may suppose Louis the Fourteenth or Charles the Second.'

His humanity was recognised when he was Prince of Wales by a writer, Lady Louisa Stuart. She wrote that he had 'an unspeakably kind heart, a genuine manliness of spirit' and 'an innate rectitude'. And later after his marriage to Charlotte, Princess of Mecklenburg Strelitz, his wife followed his advice during 'drawing-rooms' at St James's Palace to be 'civil to all'.

An example of his graciousness as a statesman can be seen in his remarks in 1785 to John Adams, the first American Minister appointed to the Court of St James, when he said, 'I will be very free with you. I was the last to consent to the separation; but the separation having been made and having become inevitable, I have always said, as I say now, that I would be the first to meet the friendship of the United States as an independent power.'

3 Audacity

Audacity augments courage; hesitation, fear.
Publius Syrus (1st century BC)

Boldness be my friend! Arm me, audacity.
William Shakespeare (1564–1616)

The ultimate risk is not taking risk.
Sir James Goldsmith (1933–1997)

One of the things that separates leadership from management is the drive to move on, to improve and to continue to develop. We describe this as audacity: the boldness and daring to shape the future. This boldness and daring relies on a number of characteristics: confidence, positive dissatisfaction, vision, thinking outside the box and taking action.

Confidence

As is our confidence, so is our capacity.
William Hazlitt, 1823

Evolutionary psychology points to the importance of confidence in establishing leadership. In a caveman world full of threat, uncertainty and danger, those that appeared to offer a solution or protection became an attractive proposition. By associating yourself with such an individual you increased the chances of survival for you and your offspring. This pattern seems to be embedded into our behaviour. People will follow a confident person, especially one who appears to offer a way out from uncertainty and turbulence. The rise of dictators provides strong and chilling evidence of how this can be manipulated to the extreme.

Bold knaves thrive without one grain of sense,
But good men starve for want of impudence.
John Dryden (1631–1700)

How would you rather be seen by others? As a cheerful positive individual, or as a negative and miserable one? Who are you most likely to be inspired to follow, an unsure and unclear individual or someone who is confident and bold? What gets things done, complaining about all the problems and the fact that they will never get fixed, or believing that there must be a solution and setting off in search of it?

There are always two creations to achieve anything, the mental creation and the physical creation. A thought precedes the action. Consequently, whatever we think conditions the actions we take and the results we experience. For this reason, the power of belief is huge. If we believe we will not be able to achieve something, it is likely we will not even try. Conversely, if we believe we can, we will try. We may not get as far as we had hoped, but we will have come much further than if we had not tried at all. It was probably this kind of thinking that prompted Henry Ford to say, 'Whether you believe you can or you can't, you're right.'

Our thoughts can become 'self-fulfilling prophecies'. Consider how your thoughts impact on your performance. If you are to present to a group of people and you think they are uninterested or even hostile, this may become the reality; your behaviour may incite these kinds of behaviour in them. If we believe in what we have to say, that it has benefits for the listeners and that they will be grateful for the insights we offer, we will appear more at ease, more confident and more credible.

The voices we listen to in our heads can have a huge impact on our lives and our results. Often we are not honest with ourselves and with others. We may say, 'I can't do that', when really what we mean is, 'I don't want to do that.' There is a big difference. 'Can't' implies a lack of ability and 'disempowers' you. What the brain hears it can easily perceive. If it hears 'can't' too often, it may easily convince you that you are of limited capability. If you have the capability to do it but not the time or inclination, the words, 'I choose not to' are more honest and empowering. If you want to boost your self-confidence and your self-esteem, ban yourself from using the word 'can't.' What we believe becomes our reality. What we dwell on tends to come about. As a consequence it benefits us to always think things in the positive. Our brain processes this more clearly. For instance, ever had the thought 'don't trip over the wire', only to find that you very expertly manage to crash to the floor with your foot tangled in it? The brain appears to be more receptive to the direct action. The 'don't' gets lost along the way and it is as though we are telling ourselves to 'trip over the wire'. A clear expression of thought is 'safely step over the wire'. This points out the positive action to the brain and does not introduce the possibility of committing that which we want to avoid.

The power of belief, combined with effort, can significantly enhance performance. This was demonstrated by William I when as Duke William aged only 19, he raised troops in Eastern Normandy to join Henry I of France in a battle against western rebels. Following this victory Duke William chaired an ecclesiastical council which imposed the extraordinary 'Truce of God' on Normandy. Under this truce it was not allowed to fight private wars on certain days (Wednesday evening to Monday morning) and during certain periods such as Lent and Pentecost. Both the Duke of Normandy and King of France were not covered by the truce, but anyone else who did not follow it was at risk of being excommunicated from the Church. The combination of the battle and the truce led to a temporary (if not enduring) victory over the rebels. It is some testimony to the confidence and power of belief of this 19-year-old duke that he carried this off.

Oliver Cromwell also used the concept of the power of belief by choosing 'the freeway' as opposed to 'the formal way'. This entailed Cromwell choosing men for his armies who really believed in the cause and were therefore totally motivated. He considered that such men would, if properly trained, equipped and remunerated, outperform soldiers/mercenaries who were just doing the job for money.

As in William's case, expectation of success stimulates and reinforces effort. Just as one tends to steer a car in the direction that one is looking, if one is focused on fear of failure, effort is diminished. If one is focused on anticipation of success, effort is enhanced. It is no coincidence that top sports people spend a lot of time training their positive thinking as well as their physical technique. Without the belief that they can win, they are unlikely to, no matter how hard they train. The effect of positive 'self-talk' and positive managerial support on performance and achievement should not be underestimated. People respond to confidence. The business world responds to confidence: the recent 'dot.com' story is a clear illustration of that.

The encouraging news is that we can 'reprogramme' ourselves. By consciously thinking positive thoughts and by deleting the negative ones we can affirm more helpful messages in our own mind. We can bolster our self-esteem and our confidence. We can present a more positive image to others, and make ourselves more attractive as a partner, friend and leader. We can start to believe that we have enormous untapped potential, and we begin to think audacious thoughts.

Positive dissatisfaction

There is a lot of dissatisfaction in the world. Individuals feel dissatisfied, teams, departments, organisations, even countries – all may experience dissatisfaction. We believe there are two types of dissatisfaction: positive dissatisfaction and negative dissatisfaction.

Positive dissatisfaction may sound like a contradiction, an oxymoron. So what do we mean? Listen to conversations at work, in the bar or in the street. Chances are you will hear a lot of negative dissatisfaction: people moaning about how bad things are but waiting for someone else to sort it out. We often call this 'BMW' – 'bitching, moaning and whining'. It serves little purpose and usually makes things worse. The best it can achieve is to help to relieve some pent-up feelings by 'getting it off your chest'. This is an important part of managing our stress. However, in terms of solving the issue, it takes us nowhere. It often makes it worse: a downward spiral of 'ain't it awful' encourages the belief that nothing can be done about it. This is disempowering for the individual and dangerous for the organisation.

Just consider a few simple examples of your own. Take filing, for instance. When faced with a pile of filing, how do you feel when you moan to a friend or colleague about how it needs doing, but it's a pain and wouldn't it be great if you could click your fingers and someone else would get rid of it? You might feel momentarily better for getting it off your chest. Your friend might join in with 'Too true, I've got a desk-full as well, can't ever imagine getting round to it.' You pick up the pace of moaning with, 'I know, when will it end? How can we be expected to cope? It's really p*****g me off!' You and your friend part and go back to your over-crowded desks, with an acute awareness of the size of the filing pile, and a heavy feeling in your heart. What you have witnessed is two people wallowing in negative dissatisfaction.

Compare this with how you feel if you plan time to do the filing and push through and do it. Not only do you feel good about the fact you can see your desk for the first time in weeks, you feel good about yourself because you took charge. You accepted responsibility for the problem and moved from negative dissatisfaction to positive dissatis-faction. You accepted responsibility and took action, and your self-esteem grew in the process.

Examples abound in all aspects of work and life, whether it is moaning about the room being too cold but not getting up and closing the windows, or that communication at work is dreadful but not suggesting improvements. Negative dissatisfaction can abound. And it can be contagious. Before you know it, a group, team, department, organisation or nation can become infected.

Progress is made by those who have 'positive dissatisfaction': a frus-tration with the current state, and a desire to reach an improved desired future state. This requires people to accept their responsibility to influence improvement. The challenge in managing ourselves is to manage our thinking so that we are always seeking solutions, not moaning about the problems. If we wait for other people to fix our problems for us we will probably die disappointed, bitter and twisted. 'If it is to be it is up to me!' There is always something we can do to improve a situation. Often we talk ourselves out of these possibilities because we assume we need to be in control of a situation in order to improve it. This is false and misleading. We cannot control events: there are too many variables. The only thing we can control are our choices. We cannot even control the results of our choices. We can choose to get the early train to arrive at work on time, but we cannot absolutely control all events to ensure that we do arrive on time. We cannot ensure that we will even get out of bed tomorrow morning, let alone control all the variables within a multinational company! However, do not despair. This may sound disempowering, but it is not. It is the reverse. If we think in terms of needing to be in control in order to be able to act, we drastically limit our potential and self-confidence. If we change our perspective and think instead of influence rather than control, our potential to take action has a much wider and deeper horizon.

We can illustrate this with the following diagrams. In the first, we only perceive two main options. We can either do something about the situation because we have the power to control decisions and events, or we cannot because we perceive ourselves to be powerless.

1

| Control | | Zero direct impact |

Figure 3.1

41

In the second diagram our either/or thinking is replaced with a spectrum of influence. In this perspective, we accept that we can never truly control events, but we have degrees of influence. At the top end of the spectrum, our influence may nudge towards 'control'. At the bottom of the spectrum our influence is very indirect, but we still have the opportunity to influence, often through others.

2 High influence · Lower influence · 10 · 1

Figure 3.2

We may well be at risk in our thinking. If situations do not seem under our control, we may disempower ourselves by automatically consigning them to the 'sod all' box. Remember, whether we believe we can or we can't, we're right.

When we are leading others our challenge is to move negative dissatisfaction into positive dissatisfaction. We need the critical mass of people dissatisfied but keen to improve things. To help your people make this move you need to provide two things, a vision of a better state, and an idea of how to get there.

Vision

> Vision is the art of seeing things invisible.
> Jonathan Swift, 1711

> He who plants a walnut tree expects not to eat the fruit.
> English proverb

> It wasn't raining when Noah built the ark.
> Anon.

> Nothing happens unless at first a dream.
> Anon.

In order to move on we need to be focused on the future, not the past. Managing our focus on the future requires us to visualise where we want, or need, to be. In order to bring other people with us into that future we need to be able to clearly articulate the desired future state. This is a test of our leadership. Leadership without a vision is worthless. Companies need vision in order to inspire employees, provide a common direction, develop and exploit potential and then optimise achievements. Individuals need vision for similar reasons: to clarify their direction, to inspire themselves, to release their full potential and therefore optimise their desired achievements.

In the more modest changes we may wish to make to our personal and/or business lives, we will consider the two aspects: personal visualisation, and articulating a vision as the foundation for change and improvement.

As a leader of change, the change should first start with ourselves. Unless we 'put our own house in order' what right do we have to expect others to change? If we are to lead by example, we need to start with ourselves. With this in mind, we will consider personal visualisation first.

The vital tool for vision is imagination: seeing what is not yet there. Albert Einstein recognised this when he said, 'Imagination is more important than knowledge.' He understood that whenever we create anything, we always create it first in thought. If we are bounded by what we experience today, we will not move forward. We will be trapped by our lack of a picture of what is possible. Leadership is all about what might be possible, a belief and a picture of a desired future state. For aspiring twenty-first century visionaries there are some practical ways to stimulate visionary thinking. Most of the historic figures featured in this book are visionaries. A prime example is Sir Christopher Wren, Britain's greatest architect. In his book *His Invention So Fertile: A life of Sir Christopher Wren*, Adrian Tinniswood writes, 'No one either then or now has ever possessed as much vision as Sir Christopher Wren. As a mathematician and astronomer, as a founder of the Royal Society, he changed the course of scientific history. As an architect he changed the face of England and the course of architectural history. To have changed the world is no small thing. If you seek his monument, look around.'

Napoleon I (Napoleon Bonaparte, Emperor of France) was also a man of great vision. His objective was for a united Europe. He wrote while in exile, 'I wished to found a European system, a European code of laws, a European judiciary ... there would be but one people in Europe.' Much has been written about Napoleon's defeat by the Duke of Wellington at the Battle of Waterloo, but many might think that with the establishment of the EEC, the European Court of Justice and the euro, it is Napoleon's dream that is being realised. When Victor Hugo, French poet, novelist and playwright, wrote of Napoleon in 1862, 'Napoleon – mighty somnambulist of a vanished dream', he might have been too hasty.

The technique of visualisation helps to clarify the picture in your head. Once the picture is clear, you may choose to mobilise people for change by clearly articulating it as a vision. The following steps help to clarify a vision, a definition of a desired future state.

First of all, think of something you would like to achieve. This could relate to work or your personal life. Go and find a quiet place where you will not be disturbed. Make yourself comfortable by sitting or lying down. Close your eyes and concentrate on your breathing. Breath slowly and deeply, from your stomach. Each time you exhale, imagine that you are allowing all the tension in your mind and body to flow out with your breath.

Now start to relax your body. You can do this by thinking about each part of your body in turn. Start at your scalp and work down to your toes. Concentrate on the particular part of your body and speak to yourself in your mind saying, my scalp is relaxing, my scalp is relaxed. Now move on to your forehead and repeat the process. Keep your breathing slow and deep all the time.

When you feel deeply relaxed, start to imagine the thing you would like. Think of it in the present tense. Imagine that you already have it. Imagine what it feels like, and how you feel about having it. If it is an object, think about how it feels. Imagine using it and showing it to others. If it is a situation, imagine yourself there in graphic detail, including tastes, smells, noises, conversations. This should take as long as feels right. Sometimes you may hold the image for a short time. On other occasions you may stay with the daydream longer, enjoying being in it. Before you leave your daydream, make a very positive statement to yourself, aloud or in your head, that seals the image in the present tense. For instance, 'I am enjoying a fantastic weekend with my friends and family', or 'My team are organised, effective and work really well together'. These affirmations are very important. They give your thoughts positive energy by suggesting that what you desire already exists or is coming to you. Focus on your vision frequently, but avoid thoughts of anger or frustration. These get in the way of the process. Your mind starts to focus on why it might not happen, rather than why it will.

On a personal level, visualisation can dramatically improve our ability to reach our full potential. It can also be very useful in clarifying where we want to get to before we begin to lead others. As we have already said, leadership without vision is worthless.

As leaders, we need a process that will help us to move ourselves, our team and our organisation forward. In order to move from the current state there needs to be dissatisfaction. However, as we have already discussed, all too often this dissatisfaction may be negative and destructive. As leaders we need to focus this into positive dissatisfaction. In order to achieve this, we need to provide two key things: a clear vision of a better state and a route map of how to achieve it. We can illustrate this with the following diagram.

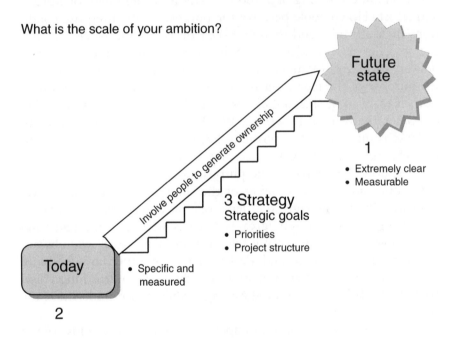

Figure 3.3 Where's your positive dissatisfaction?

Many managers spend time understanding what is happening today and striving for incremental improvements. There are two limitations to this approach. The first is that it does not successfully stimulate positive dissatisfaction. Individuals and teams are unlikely to get excited about a picture they do not see. If they do not perceive the need to change, they will choose to keep the status quo. The second limitation is that we are automatically boxing ourselves into the existing framework. We are starting with what we already have, rather than determining what we really need. Unless we free our minds and use our imagination, we are unlikely to visualise anything beyond the boundary of today's experience. This can easily limit our ambition in terms of what we believe to be possible.

The first step therefore is to develop a very clear and specific description ('vision') of the desired future state. To be useful this needs to be clear, concise, stretching and meaningful to all members of the organisation or department. Part of this process can include the clarification of the reason the organisation or department exists. This common understanding of purpose is critical for alignment of attitude and effort. How people perceive the purpose of an enterprise conditions their attitudes and therefore their decisions and behaviour. For example, let us consider a team involved in the manufacture and delivery of pizzas. Members of the team may have different views on the purpose of the team. Let us say that James perceives the purpose of their team to be 'making pizzas'. Alex however sees it as providing customers with a great service, but Katie is clear that it is about making as much profit as possible. Each of these people are keen to do well, and cares about the success of their enterprise. However, the filter of how they perceive the purpose will condition the attitudes, behaviour and decision making of the three individuals. James will evaluate things through the lens of 'making pizzas is what is important', Alex through 'great service is what is important' and Katie through 'making profit is what is important'. Each will observe the attitude, behaviour and decisions of the other in a state of confusion. This confusion over time can lead to frustration and conflict. Each believes he or she is right and cannot understand the actions of the others.

Clearly this is a simplistic example, but the principle holds true in more complex scenarios. Indeed, the greater the complexity in the situation, the more pronounced the potential problem. Departments can pursue their own perception of what is important, to the detriment of the whole organisation. Individuals lose sight of why they are at work and put effort into doing the wrong things right. People and teams can lapse into an attendance mentality: 'as long as I am at work I am fulfilling what is required of me'. For an enterprise to be successful we need people and resources focused on doing the right things right, willingly and with commitment. This is unlikely to happen if there is no clear alignment within the organisation. The ideal we should be striving for looks a little like this.

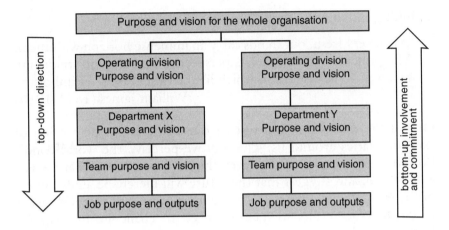

Figure 3.4 Organisational alignment

The purpose and vision need to be deduced from the needs of customers, shareholders and the marketplace. Once the initial draft has been created, all employees need to have the opportunity to understand it, discuss it and suggest improvements. This usually requires an investment in well designed and organised group workshops. People own what they help to create.

Give us a clear vision that we may know where we stand and what to stand for, because unless we stand for something, we shall fall for anything.

Once the desired future state is clear, the next step is to assess the current state position of each part of the purpose and vision. This establishes the size of the gap in each part of the purpose and vision statements. We now have the framework for deducing the strategic objectives and their relative priority. Ideally, each strategic priority should have a senior person to champion it. A project approach usually increases the opportunity of success. Each strategic objective needs an agreed plan with milestones. To gain the commitment of all employees, they all need to be included in the development of how to deliver the plans, and in their delivery. Unless they have responsibility for the development and implementation, they will have little ownership of the process. The approach taken will always need to be tailored to the circumstances and context of your organisation. A variation of this concept was designed and applied at Historic Royal Palaces, and this is set out in Part III of this book in Chapter 8.

Thinking outside the box

> When very fresh, our minds carry an immense horizon with them.
> The present image shoots its perspective far before it, irradiating
> in advance the regions in which lie the thoughts as yet unborn.
>
> William James (1842–1910)

One of the things that can restrict our vision is our perception of the boundaries around us. The way we perceive the world conditions our expectations. It can even 'make' us see things that are not really there, and suggest that the future will merely be an extension of the past. If you agree with this analysis, it follows that if we want to change the results we get, we need to challenge the way we perceive the boundaries.

Rather than perceiving events objectively or passively, we actively construct our perception from our past experiences and beliefs. Each of us can fall into the trap of believing that the way we perceive things is the only way to perceive them. It narrows our opportunities by preventing us exploring other possibilities. The more firmly fixed the beliefs and perceptions, the more we might resist or 'screen out' new ideas or alternatives. Elizabeth I showed her frustration with the closed thinking approach of puritan Dr Humphreys on her visit to Oxford in 1566 when she said, 'Mr Doctor, that loose gown becomes you so well, I wonder your notions should be so narrow.'

Such an approach was certainly not true of Prince Albert, whose Great Exhibition of 1851, itself a product of out-of-the-box thinking, encouraged such thinking in a multitude of ways. What Albert had hoped, that real change would result from the event, actually happened. It was not all a one way process, knowledge leaving Britain. A manufacturer of wood screws based in Birmingham, John Nettleford, found an American-made machine which fully mechanised the process for making screws. Until 1851 Nettlefords had made screws very inefficiently by hand, and this was to change when they adopted the American process with consequent benefit to Nettlefords and the Birmingham economy.

Another 'out of the box' idea of the Great Exhibition (or is it an 'in the box' one?) was the innovation of the 'public waiting rooms'. These 'rooms' were set up on an experimental basis at Bedford Street for ladies, and at Fleet Street for gentlemen, and they were the precursor of well-managed public lavatories. Not only did the rooms perform a function, so to speak, but they actually made a profit (on a 2 penny charge, 4 penny for a clean towel) of about £1,800 during the five months of their operation during the Exhibition period. It would appear they were well managed, as they were described as 'of so novel and delicate a character'. This is a particular opportunity for twenty-first century public lavatory providers to learn from the past.

Unlike Prince Albert, we can find our existing perceptions prevent us from seeing new relationships, different markets and creative solutions to old problems. Throughout history many major breakthroughs have been as a result of a break with traditional thinking. Columbus and other voyagers of discovery set out in the face of public opinion which expected them to fall off the edge of the world. Galileo faced opposition and persecution at the hands of religious leaders for his revelation that the earth was not the centre of the solar system, and people laughed at the idea of heavier than air flight. Sir Isaac Newton contributed to the British Enlightenment, the philosophical movement which stressed the importance of reason and the critical reappraisal of existing ideas and social institutions. Apart from being a pre-eminent process thinker, Newton was a colossal agent for change. His genius was recognised by contemporaries, and by those like Wordsworth who were to follow later. Wordsworth wrote the following description of Newton's outside the box thinking style:

> Newton with his prism and silent face,
> ... a mind forever,
> Voyaging through strange thoughts alone.

Fixed mind-sets can equip us very badly for dealing with change. They may make us too slow to adapt. We respond too late because we are fixed in yesterday's patterns of thought. Patterns of thought can easily become habit, and habits can migrate into the perception that they are the only way to do things. For example, driven by war needs, alcohol licensing laws were introduced in 1916 in the UK to encourage munitions workers to keep to their work schedules. After the war the laws continued, and shaped the social habits of the nation for 70 years.

Unless we actively examine and challenge our own thinking, our existing 'mind-sets', we may be limiting the boundaries of what is available to us. Through questioning something, we are more able to clarify our thinking on a particular subject. This may be the reason for the apparent connection between crises and creativity (something graphically demonstrated in Historic Royal Palaces in Part III, Chapter 9). The crisis may force us to adopt a new viewpoint which allows us the opportunity to 'rewrite' the boundaries and the perceived 'rules'. Why wait for the crisis? Surely it would make far greater sense to change the mind-set before the crisis, as this would probably reduce stress, inefficiency and unnecessary effort. It would make sense, but it requires courage and faith to change something that is perceived to be 'the way of doing it', especially if the new solution is untried. This is compounded further if the culture of an organisation is risk averse and blame rich! It also needs time. Unless we make time to challenge assumptions and mind-sets, we are unlikely to climb out of the mental box we have created for ourselves. We will only make time if we value it. Our belief is that all people at work are paid to think. Unfortunately most organisations do not encourage it.

Any business, large or small, is awash with mind-sets. They have management mind-sets, sales mind-sets, recruitment mind-sets, marketing mind-sets, research and development mind-sets, human resource development mind-sets. The interrelationship of all these mind-sets is crucial to the success and longevity of any culture or organisation. The crucial question is, how appropriate are these mind-sets? Are they historical remnants which do more to impede than promote improvement? Are individuals encouraged to challenge these mind-sets by searching for more suitable and effective ones? Do you as their manager or colleague actively support them in this? Managers and organisations often seek improvement by changing systems or processes, but for this to work it is the underlying thinking that must change.

It is our view that many improvement initiatives fail because the underlying thinking does not change. The implication of this is that the existing thinking and 'the system' slowly strangle the remedy. However, a combination of some short-term improvement, and the need to continue to find another 'cure' for improved performance, leads to the search and purchase of another 'quick fix' remedy, a further 'sticking plaster' appears on the body of the business.

Over a number of decades universities, directors and managers have developed a traditional way of thinking about management: a 'management mind-set'. Overall this approach was based on a few people having all the information and making all the decisions, and the workers being told what to do. This was born out of the move to mass production techniques in the early part of the twentieth century. The issue is not that this 'command and control' approach was not of value, but that we have not continued to learn. We have not learned to question the assumptions that govern the way we run our organisations.

Solutions are created for a problem at a particular point in time. As times change and the forces in that time shift, how safe is it to assume that the problem is the same, or that the thinking that gave us the original solution is still correct? In short, many of the management practices that we have come to think of as 'normal' were originally developed in response to problems of their time. Today they may be causing damage to our organisations.

In essence, therefore, we have a problem of management thinking. Unless managers change the way they think, their system will not change and therefore its performance will not change. This is the real challenge of leadership.

Taking action

> Sit, walk or run
> Just don't wobble.
>> Zen saying

> The test of any man lies in action.
>> Pindar (5th century BC)

The true test of leadership and of audacity is in the actions that are taken. There should be no prizes for having the best plan, but there should be prizes for implementing the plan. Perhaps surprisingly the Merry Monarch, King Charles II, was a man of action. His prize was saving the Tower of London. He personally went to the Tower (by water) during the Great Fire of London. Here he oversaw the creation of a fire break by the demolition of a number of houses. If it were not for this swift and decisive action the Tower of London would have been among the 13,200 buildings destroyed in the fire. And Charles did not just command from horseback. He joined in the arduous fire fighting work himself, wielding a bucket and spade, and he encouraged his courtiers to do the same. When his fire fighting stint ended his clothes were soaking, his face black and he was covered in mud and dirt.

If we demonstrate and encourage confidence, stimulate positive dissatisfaction, clarify a vision and challenge existing mind-sets by 'thinking outside the box', it will come to nought if we fail to act. Indeed, it may well make things worse as expectations have been raised.

To get different results we have to do things differently or do different things. We have to act, not just talk. This may require us to constructively confront some of our personal and corporate mind-sets. It may ask us to begin discussing the perceived 'undiscussable' items. We may need to take difficult decisions to remove obstacles to improvement. Most of all, it may need us to talk with individuals who are known to be holding the organisation back from achieving its full potential. We need to act on the difficult issues. But we need to act with integrity, being true to our values, and with graciousness. All of this requires moral courage, for it is easier to leave things the way they are.

Tenacity, persistence, perseverance are part of the action subset. Continued, steady belief and effort, withstanding difficulty or discouragement are critical for success.

Sir Christopher Wren displayed tenacity in the building of St Paul's Cathedral: although frustrated by frequent requests for changes, he prepared six designs before eventual approval and oversaw a 36-year design and build timetable. Prince Albert also showed persistence with his reform of Buckingham Palace and the creation and management of the Great Exhibition, described in Chapter 4 of this book.

To illustrate persistence we can call on Euphens who in 1579 said, 'Many strokes overthrow the tallest oaks', and George Bernard Shaw, who wrote, 'I don't believe in circumstances. The people who get on in this world are the people who get up and look for the circumstances they want, and if they can't find them, make them.'

 ## Audacity: key points

- People will follow a confident person, especially one who appears to offer a way out from uncertainty and turbulence.
- Whatever we think conditions the actions we take and the results we experience.
- If you want to boost your self-confidence and your self-esteem, ban yourself from using the word 'can't'.
- What we believe becomes our reality.

- What we dwell on tends to come about.
- Whether we believe we can or we can't, we're right.
- As a consequence it benefits us to always think things in the positive.
- Progress is made by those who have 'positive dissatisfaction': a frustration with the current state, and a desire to reach an improved desired future state.
- This requires you to accept your responsibility to influence improvement.
- The challenge is to manage our thinking so that we are always seeking solutions, not moaning about the problems.
- The only thing we can control are our choices (we cannot even control the results of our choices).
- When we are leading others our challenge is to move negative dissatisfaction into positive dissatisfaction.
- We need the critical mass of people dissatisfied but keen to improve things.
- To help your people make this move you need to provide two things, a vision of a better state, and an idea of how to get there.
- Leadership without a vision is worthless.
- As leaders of change, we should start the change with ourselves. Unless we put our own house in order, what right do we have to expect others to change?
- Visualisation can dramatically improve our ability to reach our full potential.
- Common understanding of purpose is critical for alignment of attitude and effort. How people perceive the purpose of an enterprise conditions their attitudes and therefore their decisions and behaviour.
- The purpose and vision need to be deduced from the needs of customers, shareholders and the marketplace.
- People own what they help to create.
- One of the things that can restrict our vision is our perception of the boundaries around us. The way we perceive the world conditions our expectations.
- Each of us can fall into the trap of believing that the way we perceive things is the only way to perceive them.

- Our existing perceptions can prevent us seeing new relationships, different markets and creative solutions to old problems.
- The more firmly fixed our beliefs and perceptions, the more we might resist or 'screen out' new ideas or alternatives.
- Fixed mind-sets can equip us very badly for dealing with change. They may make us too slow to adapt. We respond too late because we are fixed in yesterday's patterns of thought.
- Unless we make time to challenge assumptions and mind-sets, we are unlikely to climb out of the mental box we have created for ourselves.
- Many improvement initiatives fail because the underlying thinking does not change.
- Many of the management practices that we have come to think of as 'normal' were originally developed in response to problems of their time. Today they may be causing damage to our organisations.
- In essence, therefore, we have a problem of management thinking.
- Unless managers change the way they think, their system will not change and therefore its performance will not change. This is the real challenge of leadership.
- The true test of leadership, and of audacity, is in the actions that are taken. We have to act, not just talk.
- To get different results we have to do things differently or do different things.
- But we need to act with integrity, being true to our values, and with graciousness.
- All of this requires moral courage for it is easier to leave things the way they are.

Audacity toolbox

1 *Managing our thoughts*

Negative and self-limiting thoughts have a habit of creeping into our minds, especially when we are stressed or distressed. To keep our thoughts focused on what we want, rather than what we fear, requires effort. Affirmations can be a great help here.

Rather than allowing our thoughts to be conditioned entirely by our subconscious fears, or our memory-driven 'filters', we can 'reprogramme' our minds in the positive. An affirmation is simply a clear and concise statement of what we want to be. We repeat it often in our heads to reinforce what we want to dwell on, so that this has a better chance to become our reality. For example, if we have a tendency to feel tense and anxious, a positive affirmation to counter this might be, 'I am a calm and confident person, now and at all times.' The frequent repetition of this phrase, aloud or in our heads, will assist the promotion of this behaviour. If we can learn to feel the onset of our anxiety and tenseness at the early stages, we can use the affirmation to prevent tenseness and anxiety taking hold.

In addition, to remove negative thoughts we can 'speak to ourselves' to delete the negative thought and replace it with a positive affirmation. For instance, if we experience the thoughts and feelings of 'I am tired and miserable', we could think, 'Delete that thought. I am energetic and cheerful.' This could be further affirmed during the day by regularly using, 'I am an energetic and cheerful person.'

Now we know that some of you will be thinking that this sounds a bit weird. You may even feel it is foolish. However, if we continue to do what we have always done, we are likely to get the results we have always got. So, like everything else in this book, and in life, the choice is yours. There is something really important we would like to point out here. As all of this happens in your head, you can do it and no one will ever know! Why not be daring and have a go?

2 Personal reflection

Most people have self-limiting and self-defeating thoughts. These may be a result of previous experience, or a lack of self-confidence, or both. For example, if you missed one or two key lessons at school, let us say in French, you may have struggled to keep up. Even worse, you may have developed a block due to mild panic. This belief may then hold you back from practising and experimenting with the French language throughout your life, as you have grown to believe that you 'cannot do French'. This is a self-limiting belief based on past experience and driven by memory.

Find somewhere quiet to sit and think through the following question.

What are some of the self-limiting and self-defeating thoughts that you feel are holding you back from achieving happiness or your full potential?

List them on a separate sheet.

Now develop positive affirmations for each of these self-limiting and self-defeating thoughts. Your affirmations need to be clear, concise and expressed in the present tense. For example, 'I am a positive and energetic person,' not, 'I want to be positive and energetic.'

Set out a grid on a separate sheet of paper designed as follows:

Self-limiting and self-defeating thoughts	Positive affirmations to counter them

We suggest that you choose one area at a time to begin with. Choose the affirmation you want to work with. Work with it for a while, and then add another, and then another, and then ...

3 Personal visualisation

Plan 45 minutes' personal time in a quiet, private, relaxing location. Identify a result in your life that you deeply want to achieve. Carefully consider why you desire it and what it will bring you if you have it. Changes always bring other consequences with them. Be sure to think this through.

Start by bringing yourself into a reflective frame of mind; let go of any tension. Close your eyes and concentrate on your breathing. Breathe slowly and deeply, from your stomach. Each time you exhale, imagine that you are allowing all the tension in your mind and body to flow out with your breath.

Now start to relax your body. You can do this by thinking about each part of your body in turn. Start at your scalp and work down to your toes. Concentrate on the particular part of your body and speak to yourself in your mind saying, my scalp is relaxing, my scalp is relaxed. Now move on to your forehead and repeat the process. Keep your breathing slow and deep all the time.

When you feel deeply relaxed, start to imagine achieving a result in your life that you deeply desire. Ignore how 'possible' or 'impossible' this vision seems.

Imagine yourself accepting it into your life.

Describe, in your thoughts:

- what it looks like
- what it feels like
- how you are now that you have it.

Allow these images to wash around in your mind, whilst staying relaxed. Then ask yourself this:

This, or something better, is available to me. Do I want to take it?

Make sure you have thought clearly about this last point before you answer with a strong 'yes' to yourself.

4 Developing a business vision

Find a quiet area to work in where you will not be disturbed. Plan to take 30 minutes to complete the following questions. (Stop after 30 minutes and take a break. Revisit your work later, or on another day.)

Part A

What is the purpose of your area of responsibility (team/department/company)?

Part B

Choose a point in the future (say, three years from today). Answer each of the following questions by imagining what you will see when the vision becomes reality and write this down using the present tense ('we are ...', 'we have ...' 'customers say ...' 'employees are ...' and so on).

1. What will your customers be saying about the service from, and the performance of, your area of responsibility (team/department/company)?
2. How will employees be behaving in your area of responsibility (team/department/company)?
    *   What will they be doing that is different from today?
    *   How will they be working with each other that is different from today?
    *   What will it feel like to work in this team/department/company?
    *   How will people's conversation be different from the way it is today?
3. What will your suppliers be saying about the performance of your area of responsibility (team/department/company)?
4. What will your manager, your shareholders or stakeholders be saying about the service from, and the performance of, your area of responsibility (team/department/company)?

Timeless Management historical illustrations

Timeless Manager 3: Oliver Cromwell – audacity

Oliver Cromwell (1599–1658), English soldier and statesman.

Connections with Historic Royal Palaces

Despite being leader of the new English Republic, Oliver Cromwell made ample use of the royal palaces left empty after the execution of Charles I. Once he had been made Lord Protector (de facto king), Cromwell and his wife moved in to the royal apartments at both Whitehall and Hampton Court. At Whitehall Cromwell used the Banqueting House as his main audience chamber, and here he received foreign envoys and formal petitions. His first audience in the Banqueting House was held in March 1654, when Cromwell was attended by the ambassador of the Estates-General of Holland.

In many ways, Cromwell lived very much as a king at Hampton Court: he often hunted in the park, and made sure that the jewel in Charles I's collection of paintings, the Mantegna series *The Triumphs of Caesar*, was not sold but remained on display at the palace. In 1657 Cromwell's youngest daughter, Mary, was married in the Tudor chapel within the palace.

Historical illustration

When Oliver Cromwell died in 1658 it was during a terrible storm. His enemies at the time said it was the devil coming for his soul. On the return to the throne of King Charles II, the supporters of his father dug up the body of Cromwell from its burial place in Westminster Abbey and hung it from a gallows at Tyburn before eventually reburying it in a deep pit. Such was the loathing of the Lord Protector of England, Scotland and Ireland by some. And yet Milton famously described him as 'Our Chief of Men'.

Since that time there have been a number of differing evaluations of Cromwell. To some he is a brutal war criminal responsible for butchering 3,000 soldiers in Ireland after they had surrendered and disarmed. To others he is the nation's saviour because he sowed the seeds of what would eventually become Britain's parliamentary democracy. Whatever his negative attributes and however they are judged by twenty-first century standards, one important element in his success was his audacity. Despite a deep sense of unworthiness this hypochondriac often acted decisively, took risk and was a (religious) visionary. He was driven to create a country that was 'disciplined in the ways of God'. God help anyone who stood in his way. He certainly lived up to his personal motto: *pax quaeritor bello* (let peace be sought through war).

There is strong evidence that Cromwell went through a spiritual and possibly mental crisis and renaissance in his twenties. Following this he considered himself 'born again' and as a result appeared to gain a greater understanding of his personal limitations and strengths. It is probably this profound self-knowledge, along with the belief that he and God were acting in tandem and therefore he could never be wrong, that led to his audacious approach. For him risk and action could never result in failure as God was always by his side. Cromwell's faith appeared genuine. He certainly convinced many of his contemporaries that he was doing God's work. Therefore, it is not surprising that among other less flattering nicknames he was known as 'God's Englishman'.

Two particular examples, among many, of his audacity and propensity for risk and action occurred at significant points in both Cromwell's career and in the history of England.

As the war of words between Parliament and King simmered and finally boiled over in 1642, Cromwell (then an obscure back-bencher) acted to prepare himself and others for war. He decided to leave London and return to the fen lands of his birth to rally local resistance to the King and his supporters. On 10 August he and his brother-in-law, Valentine Walton, led a small troop of soldiers in seizing for Parliament the arms and ammunition stockpiled in Cambridge Castle. He also intercepted and stopped an armed escort taking money and silver plate from Cambridge University to the King at York. These were brave and audacious actions, all the more remarkable since the war did not officially begin until 22 August when the King raised his standard at Nottingham. If the problems between King and Parliament had been resolved, as seemed possible in these early days, Cromwell could have found himself arraigned on charges of robbery and treason.

Cromwell's capacity to move quickly and strike while allies were undecided and enemies were unprepared is also well illustrated in his controversial suppression of the armed mutiny at Burford. In 1649 Parliament, having executed King Charles I, resolved to send the Army to Ireland to crush the only remaining Royalist resistance and remove the possibility of a back door invasion by Charles Stuart (Charles II). Unfortunately many in the army were not happy with this plan. Soldiers had not received their arrears of pay, and so-called Leveller radicals feared that with the army in Ireland, Parliament would backtrack on promises of political and religious reform. Leveller-inspired mutinies broke out at Banbury and Southampton. Cromwell and Fairfax set out to deal with the problem. Cromwell put in hand plans to resolve the arrears of pay issue, and addressed the troops directly, assuring them that he was 'resolved to live and die with them'. The main part of the mutiny was quelled, but members of Reynold's regiment set off to join with fellow mutineers at Salisbury.

On Sunday 13 May the mutineers entered Burford and decided to encamp for the night. Acting on intelligence reports received,

Cromwell and his troops rode through the night the 45 miles to Burford. The attack under cover of darkness completely overwhelmed the mutineers. A few of the mutineers were killed in the initial attack and 400 were disarmed and locked in the church at Burford. The ring leaders were shot in the churchyard later in the week.

In September 1650 Cromwell and his army of about 11,000 physically sapped and no doubt dispirited men were being pursued by a superior Scottish army of over double their size. It appeared that the Scottish commander, Leslie, had manoeuvred Cromwell at Dunbar into a position impossible to escape from, hemmed in by the North Sea in one direction and other routes blocked by Leslie's men. But a decision was taken by the Scots, apparently by a committee (Committee of the Estates) and not singly by Leslie, to redeploy troops into a position which Cromwell and Colonel John Lambert considered foolish and offered up opportunities for escape and much more.

Cromwell and Lambert conceived a plan to exploit the self-imposed Scottish tactical weakness. Meanwhile the Scots, cocky and comforted by their numerical supremacy, relaxed and slept during the night to prepare for the massacre they thought would follow. Cromwell had other ideas. He prepared his troops to attack and this they did, probably at about 4.00 am in the morning while the unprepared Scottish army still slept.

Apart from his conception of the plan, Cromwell's generalship was key to its success. He ensured reserve troops were engaged at exactly the right place and time. Remarkably, the result of these actions was not merely escape but thrashing of a numerically much greater enemy. Cromwell described the victory as being 'made by the Lord of Hosts as stubble to their swords' and 'his most auspicious day'. The English took 10,000 prisoners and killed 3,000 men. Audacity indeed.

Timeless Manager 4: Queen Elizabeth I – positive dissatisfaction

Queen Elizabeth I (1533–1603), known as the Virgin Queen and later Good Queen Bess, the daughter of Henry VIII by his second wife, Anne Boleyn.

Connections with Historic Royal Palaces

Queen Elizabeth stayed at the Tower of London on two occasions, at times which marked the lowest and the highest points in her life.

In February 1554 Elizabeth was brought to the Tower as a prisoner and suspected traitor on the orders of her sister Mary. She spent several terrifying months detained in the royal lodgings at the Tower, waiting to hear whether or not Mary would prosecute her. Five years later, on Mary's death, Elizabeth came again to the Tower, as acknowledged and celebrated queen, and stayed in the castle on the eve of her coronation.

Elizabeth knew her father's palace of Hampton Court extremely well. Here, as a child of four, she had carried the robe of her brother, later Edward VI, in his christening procession in 1537. As Queen, Elizabeth continued to come to Hampton Court frequently, though she almost died of smallpox at Hampton Court in 1562. In 1564 Sir James Melville, the envoy of Mary Queen of Scots, visited Elizabeth at Hampton Court. Here Elizabeth plied Melville with questions about how she compared with Mary, as he recorded in his memoirs: 'She [Elizabeth] next desired to know of me what colour of hair was reputed the best, and whether my queen's hair or hers was fairest?', to which Melville diplomatically made the reply, 'You are the fairest Queen in England, and mine is the fairest Queen in Scotland.'

Historical illustration

Before her coming of age the father she adored had ordered the execution of her mother, she was publicly labelled a bastard, abused by her stepfather and imprisoned in the Tower of London, fearful of losing her own head. So it is hardly surprising that when Queen Elizabeth I emerged from her coronation at Westminster Abbey she had more than just a crown on her head: she was imbued with the trait of positive dissatisfaction.

As monarch this trait first evidenced itself early, at the opening of her first Parliament, when Sir Nicholas Bacon, Lord Keeper of the Great Seal, speaking on her behalf told of her desire not to 'bring any bondage or servitude to her people, or give any just occasion to them of any inward grudge or tumults or stirs might arise as hath done of late days'. In his book *Elizabeth: Apprenticeship*, Dr David Starkey referred to Bacon's address as Elizabeth's mission statement. During the 44 years and 4 months of her reign she certainly tried to live by it, by resolutely challenging the old paradigm: that conflict, violence and war were the most effective methods of handling dispute and difference. She always chose reason and logic over extremism, until the last years of her reign, when circumstances forced a changed approach. She would infuriate even her most ardent supporters by not reaching quick decisions, preferring to think things through. But when she wanted to she could decide and act quickly.

An example of this was when she reduced her influential Privy Council from 40 to 20, thus streamlining decision making and feedback. She saw this as a prerequisite to governing effectively.

Another key requirement to ensure that her mission was achieved was simply to stay in power. Of course, she assumed power in a sexist age, at a time when women were not expected to assume leadership roles, and it was highly fashionable to plot against the monarchy. And the way in which her half-sister Mary I had ruled before her had confirmed to her people the inappropriateness of female monarchy.

Her femininity was a real stumbling block to her continuing desire for power in other ways. She understood that the choice of a husband who might please one faction but anger another, and the sex of her child, or indeed a childless marriage, could have a disastrous effect on her reputation and therefore her power base. She must have also been highly sceptical of the chances for marriage to be successful, given the track record of her father (two divorces, two 'terminations', one death in childbirth), and her cousin, Mary Queen of Scots (three failed marriages). When it came to the crunch her desire for power won over the need for love and companionship.

Despite numerous suitors she remained unmarried, the 'Virgin Queen', and this undoubtedly enhanced her reputation with the people and enabled her to focus on monarchy. She did this by applying her undoubted intellectual skills and learning. She had been taught by the finest tutors from Cambridge University and was fluent in six languages, including Greek and Latin.

The effect of her dissatisfaction with previous extremist styles of settling issues can be seen in the way in which, at least initially, Elizabeth handled potentially polarising and extremely sensitive religious conflicts. The context for this work was a Europe beset by religious turmoil and, in England, unhelpful legacies from both her father and half-sister. They had preferred to deal with conflict by the use of force and violence.

Elizabeth's natural inclination was to choose a more moderate approach, allowing the issues to be debated in a way that avoided extremes in order to achieve a unifying outcome. In 1577 the English chronicler, Raphael Holinshed, compared Elizabeth's approach with that of her half-sister: 'After all the stormy, tempestuous, and blustering windy weather of Queen Mary was overblown ... it pleased God to send England calm and quiet season, a clear and lovely sunshine, a quitset from former broils of a turbulent estate, and a world of blessings by good Queen Elizabeth.'

This new operating method was evidenced in a number of ways, including Queen Elizabeth respecting the right of her people to hold their own religious beliefs (at least during the early part of her reign). Francis Bacon succinctly interpreted this aspect of her style: 'Not liking to make windows into men's souls and secret thoughts'.

Although a Protestant, Elizabeth demonstrated her tolerance of Catholicism right at the start of her reign by continuing the appointment of three Catholics on her first Council, and the subsequent appointment of Sir James Croft, also a Catholic. She disliked extremism, particularly in connection with religious beliefs. This showed itself in her regular beratings of Sir Francis Walsingham about his extremist Protestant views and also of her cousin Sir Francis Knollys who expressed similar views. She tried to keep a 'middle way' for which she was criticised. She employed Dr John Bull as her chapel organist and other Catholics such as William Byrd and Thomas Tallis, all for their talent regardless of religious beliefs.

In 1559, early in her monarchy, her moderation can be seen in the way she dealt with the establishment of the Church of England in the Anglican Faith by the passing of the Acts of Supremacy and Uniformity. These Acts dealt with confirming her as Head of the Church of England, and changes to the church service which were fundamental to defining the two faiths. She agreed to a number of compromises to get the Acts through the Lords, including changing her title from 'Supreme Head of the Faith' to less controversial but also less prestigious 'Governor of the Faith'.

Her abandonment of the harsh and divisive approaches of her half-sister and father in dealing with dissidents can be seen in the type of penalties that were included in the Acts. She preferred to opt for fines, loss of office or imprisonment rather than torture and beheading. The compromises that resulted from the process did not please everyone. In fact it was difficult to find anyone who was pleased by the Acts, but then neither side was so displeased that they took drastic action to usurp them.

The middle-of-the-road Queen tried really hard to continue with her inclusive approach, and she must have been very disappointed that events were to force her to adopt a different, harsher style towards the end of her reign.

There is some difference of view among historians as to Elizabeth's real contribution to English and world history and how much of it was due to luck, for example weather conditions impacting on the victory over the Spanish Armada, or coincidence, in the flourishing of the arts, particularly the literary contribution from the likes of Shakespeare during her reign. But the boss must take some credit. Her early learning, educational prowess and love of languages surely had some impact on the cultural development of the time. The English language itself had grown by a factor of six to 24,000 in the number of words available to England's playwrights and poets during her monarchy, and learning had become fashionable.

By the time of her death, England had developed as a major maritime power ready for a subsequent world-leading role as Empire builder. The stability she created gave the nation breathing space to develop and grow and transform itself from a medieval to a Renaissance country and a latent world power. This stability was based on her reasoned approach and refusal to continue to follow the same processes as her predecessors, hoping for a different outcome: positive dissatisfaction with the status quo.

Dr Starkey summarised the promises she made in her first Parliament in two sentences: 'I will not be like my sister Mary. And I will not rule like her either.' She certainly kept these promises.

4 Focus

We must find a way or make one.
Hannibal (247–182 BC)

There is never enough time or resources to do everything. The effective individual works out what is important and focuses on it relentlessly.

Rahal Bajaj, Chairman of India's Bajaj Auto Company, believes focus is the reason the company he took control of in 1968 with an annual production capacity of about 20,000 two-wheeled vehicles grew to an output of 400,000 units a year within a 20-year period. To achieve focus we need to draw heavily on character and audacity. However, these qualities need to be supplemented with what we believe to be the vital ingredients for focus. These are a passion for simplicity, the pursuit of root causes, process thinking, and planning and review.

Simplicity

Simplify, simplify.
H. D. Thoreau (1954)

Manifest plainness, embrace simplicity.
Lao-tsu (*c.* 604–*c.* 531 BC)

Complexity is inefficient. It wastes time, materials and mental energy and causes stress, anxiety frustration and disillusionment. Many managers and organisations appear to love complexity. When faced with a choice between the simple and the complex, complexity prevails. Perhaps it is driven by a belief that something cannot be worthy unless it is complicated and difficult. This certainly appears to be the model adopted and promoted by many academic institutions and consultancies. However, it is our view that there is never any justification for things being complex when they could be simple. Complexity distracts and dissipates effort. Simplicity focuses it.

67

Complexity creeps up on us. As things evolve, they are adapted and bastardised, becoming more complex. Those who grow up with this get used to the complexity and no longer notice it. Within a relatively short space of time a process or procedure can become distorted from its original purpose. Rather than start again and redesign it for simplicity and effectiveness, the 'easy' option is taken: more alterations are added, and yet another layer of complexity is built in.

Simplicity itself is not simple. Indeed it is often a challenge to find the simplest and most effective way to do something. In order to do this we have to learn to value simplicity more highly, just as Sir Christopher Wren did in his enthusiasm early in his life for 'the Simplest Way'. Wren was to take this thinking on simplicity with him through his career (although some might argue that his English Baroque architectural style was far from simple), even when it was to his own apparent detriment. In the summer of 1658 he prepared a draft paper on a theory he had developed 'concerning the Body of Saturn and its Phases'. The following year Wren heard about the work of Huygens, a Dutch scientist, who had developed a rival theory. Although the work of Huygens did not negate the work of Wren, Sir Christopher readily admitted his preference for his rival's work because of 'the neatness and Natural simplicity of the Contrivance ... that I loved the Invention (Huygens's) beyond my owne.'

There appears to be a great irony in management thinking and organisational life. Far higher value is placed on cost than on simplicity. Yet complexity is a major source of cost. No wonder we appear mad to many of our employees. As leaders, we need to value simplicity and encourage this value in our colleagues. We need to challenge complexity, and challenge people to find simpler ways to get work done. However, it is important to avoid being simplistic. Simplicity is the art of finding the simplest way to achieve the required results. It is the art of effectiveness. Losing sight of our purpose and the results we need to achieve can lead us to go too far. We cut costs but damage the result.

This is pointless and can be costly. If we perform inconsistently and disappoint customers, we are likely to lose them. Many organisations appear over-concerned with cost control, with apparently little consideration of the implications for process effectiveness and customer satisfaction. This is a short-term game and is not consistent with creating long-term value for shareholders, customers and employees. Perhaps it stems from confusion over the difference between efficiency and effectiveness? We can be efficient in what we do. However, unless what we do is of value, we are not being effective. It is not sufficient to 'do things right', we need to be doing 'the right things right'. Similarly, prior to simplifying something we need to fully understand how a process works before we mess with it. If we act without understanding, we run the risk of being a simpleton.

Process thinking

> Endlessly following the same process,
> hoping for a different result = insanity.
>   Einstein (1879–1955)

The process we follow always heavily influences the results we experience. If we want a different result, we need to do things differently, or do different things. All else is a form of wishful thinking. The process is concerned with how we deliver the results. If we want a different result, we need to change or improve the process to give us that result. Our experience suggests to us that most organisations and managers are under-aware of the importance of process thinking. Instead, thinking is dominated by financial 'whats', with insufficient attention to asking 'why' and 'how'. Without first asking 'why', we can engage in unnecessary and wasteful activities. Without asking 'how', we are likely to tolerate inefficiencies. Asking 'Why' encourages us to focus on being effective. Asking 'how' prompts us to challenge the process, to find the simplest and most efficient way of achieving the required result.

Process thinking, as a way of life, helps us to challenge ourselves and others to obtain clarity on why we need to do something, what we need to achieve, and how to achieve it with the minimum use of resources and maximum consistency. It is the very heart of effective leadership and management. It is of paramount importance that managers both manage and develop the processes in their organisation. Managing processes is a key part of the shift from 'managing by rules and procedures' to 'managing by principles and philosophy'. Those two statements flag the importance of managing processes, but we need to explore what that means. We should start with the distinction between content and process. For example, if we examine the interactions in a small group there is a confusing mixture, but with care we can divide them into two groups:

Content: this is the 'what' of the conversation. If the topic of the meeting is 'cost control', then the 'what' items will be money, accounting, targets, allocations, costs, and so on.

Process: this is 'how' the group are working together. How are we going to work on this topic; how will we know when we are finished; how are we going to review all the figures; how will we decide? Then, as the meeting proceeds: how are we talking, listening, deciding, disagreeing, checking, handling conflict; how efficient is the meeting; how are we treating each other?

We are normally educated and trained to be very aware of the content of the conversation or problem solving and to put most, if not all, of our effort into it. By learning to diagnose process we can balance our awareness of interest in content and process. Most energy ineffectiveness in meetings and organisations is in inefficient processes.

To assist the habit of process thinking it is useful to have a framework. You can apply this mental model as a way of life. You can use it

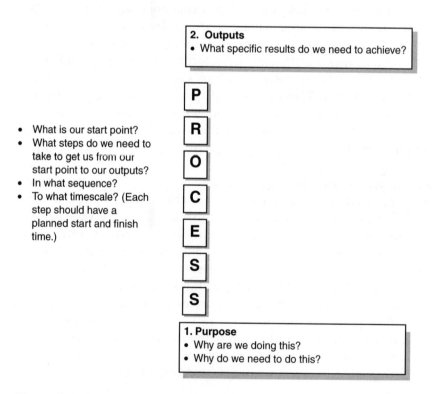

Figure 4.1 Process thinking framework

with others to encourage them to challenge the existing way of doing things, and to find improvements. It can be used to drive out 'non-value adding' activities, and to simplify 'the way the work works'. More fundamentally, it is a powerful way to encourage people to question exactly why they are engaged in doing what they do. The framework is shown opposite.

Let us further analyse the three components of process thinking.

1 *Purpose*

The start point is to have clarity on why we are doing something, or why we need to do it. Without this clarity we waste time, effort and resources. This is crucial to align people's effort to what really matters. For example, the way people perceive the purpose of their job entirely conditions their behaviour and the decisions they make. If accountants perceive the purpose of their role as being 'bean counters' that is how they will behave. Conversely, if they see their role as providing advice and support to assist their internal customers to make more informed decisions, this would guide their behaviour.

A clear and mutual understanding of purpose is critical to individual and organisation success. If a manager and a team member have different understandings of the purpose of a role, it can lead to conflict and a gross misuse of time and resources. People may also assume that the purpose of their job is static. This is not the case. An organisation exists in an ever-changing marketplace. Its strategy needs to change in order to prepare for, and adapt to, these changes. As a consequence, people's perception of their purpose needs to reflect and align with the purpose of the organisation. One of the key challenges in leading organisational change is to achieve acceptance by employees of the need for change. People will often intellectually understand the necessity for organisational change. However, this is very different from them translating this into what they specifically need to do differently. Without this fundamental shift in thinking regarding the purpose and outputs of their job, they are likely to continue to do what they have always done.

It is our belief that many people at work have never truly had their purpose explained to them. If you ask people 'What is the purpose of your job?', they will often reply by describing the main activity they perform. For instance, a butcher might say 'I sell meat.' However, this describes what he/she does, not why he/she needs to do it. To explain the purpose of being a butcher it is necessary to explain why the butcher sells meat. This is likely to involve 'To make a profit by providing customers with quality meat products and a friendly and reliable service.'

2 *Outputs*

When we are clear about the purpose, that is, why we are/need to do something, we progress on to define the specific results we need in order to fulfil our purpose. These should be measurable so that there is little argument over whether they have been achieved. Where possible, the measures should reflect a balance of requirements such as quantity, quality, time, cost and behaviour. The outputs are deduced from the purpose. So, to continue the example of butchers, we have defined their purpose as 'To make a profit by providing customers with quality meat products and a friendly and reliable service.' Critical outputs therefore are profit, quality meat products and friendly and reliable service.

Clear measures can be applied to each output to specify the exact nature of the outputs that are needed. For example:

- a profit margin of 10 per cent
- performance within hygiene regulations and quality standards for the selection and presentation of meat products
- regular customers representing at least 60 per cent of the total customer base
- at least ten discussions per week with customers to understand what they value in a butcher.

3 *Process*

Having clarified the 'why' and the 'what', we can now move on to the 'how.' How do we need to organise and work in order to deliver the 'what' with minimum stress and resources? So far, purpose and outputs have helped us to understand what we need to focus on to be effective. How we design and execute the process will determine our efficiency.

Using our example, the butcher should determine the key activities he/she must engage in to deliver the required outputs. Once these activities have been identified, processes can be developed for the consistent, effective and efficient performance of each of them. For instance, to achieve profit it will be necessary to manage costs and encourage sales. This suggests that there is a need to design processes (or review existing processes) for:

- buying
- stock management
- marketing/sales.

Process thinking can be applied to all things, at all levels. It can be used to design organisations and processes, projects and meetings. It can be applied to your life. After all, if we are unclear on the purpose of our life, how do we know what the important outputs are in the time we have? Without this, how do we effectively choose how to spend our time and design our 'process for living'?

Process thinking is an essential habit for 'focus'. It is also a key tool for achieving simplicity. Over time, processes are added to and twisted. It is the process that needs simplifying.

Causes

> Nothing comes from nothing.
> Lucretius (1st century BC)

> Every why hath a wherefore.
> Shakespeare, *The Comedy of Errors* (1592–93)

The next component of 'focus' addresses understanding the problem before attempting to find a solution. A strong focus on solving a problem without understanding the causes is likely to drive us to choose an inappropriate solution. Analysis needs to precede action.

Two of our Timeless Managers, Wren and Newton, were scientists. They used scientific method to first identify a problem, and then through observations, experiments or use of other data, find the cause and construct or test a theory to solve the problem.

In 1678 in a debate at the Royal Society on respiration, a member raised the work by Descartes which suggested that otters could hold their breath for long periods underwater because the heart of the otter contains a special opening. Wren told the meeting, which he chaired, that this was not an accurate theory since he had investigated this cause by dissecting an otter and found that no such opening existed.

The genius Newton invented a scientific method himself, which is set out at the back of this chapter as an example of process thinking. This gave structure to scientific reasoning.

In setting out these examples we are not suggesting you need to cut up otters or that the ability or skills of Wren or Newton are required! All we are suggesting is the application of basic common sense to the point where it becomes common practice.

Far too often, people make assumptions that are invalid, and jump to solutions that turn out to be wasteful of effort and resources in the long run. What we need to value is the relationship between cause and effect. Short-term thinking, convenience, pressure and human nature easily combine to encourage us to solve the effect, not the root cause(s). In other words, we address the presenting symptom. If we treat this, the situation improves temporarily but slowly grows back, as the real root causes are still present. Unless we search out and understand the root causes, we have not focused on solving the problem, just the manifestation of the problem.

Queen Elizabeth I exemplified the need for a cool and calm approach to problem solving. She eschewed the usual solutions of the sixteenth century – force of arms and war – in favour of diplomacy based on thinking and logic. She chided her more bellicose military leaders such as Sir Francis Drake 'not to suffer themselves to be transported with any haviour of vain-glory'.

Consider the person who is stressed through over-work. Taking two weeks off to rest and recuperate will help the individual recover. It will address the effect. However, if he/she returns to the same job, in the same circumstances, the chances of the stress returning are high. To solve the problem we need to understand the causes of the stress. Is it a temporary increase in work that is causing the effect, or is there a fundamental flaw in the design of the job? Is it a skills issue, or are the processes the person works in badly designed? Unless we analyse the situation we are unlikely to identify the root causes. Similar thinking manifests itself in many other ways. It is easy for individuals and organisations to see only half of the picture when pursuing performance improvement.

We can easily become locked into an unhelpful paradox. In the hope of achieving fast results with minimum investment we seek quick-fix solutions. This encourages us to purchase 'remedies'. These often come in complex packages with names like 'enterprise resource planning', 'business process re-engineering' 'the empowered organisation', and many others that you will be familiar with. Why is it that many of these initiatives fail to deliver their promise? It is our belief that these approaches are valid, but they are drained by our performance paradox. To escape this we suggest that we need to take a much more fundamental look at performance.

It is our view that many improvement initiatives fail because:

- the causes of the performance problem are not identified and understood
- the problem and the solution are treated in isolation, rather than as part of a complex and interdependent system
- the underlying thinking does not change.

There can be a number of consequences arising from these three points. Firstly, a lot of time and money can be wasted on applying or buying the wrong solution. If we experience the effects, are under pressure to fix it, and are exposed to the 'latest' fix, we might fall into the trap of buying a 'flavour of the month' remedy.

Second, cause and effect analysis suggests that there will be multiple causes to an effect, and that these causes are not limited by functional geography. Often the causes occur in distant parts of the organisation from the one where the effect manifests itself. A problem of insufficient sales might not be caused by a poor sales force. The root causes might be in poor product design, poor manufacturing quality, late delivery or poor pricing. Replacing the sales force, or sending them on expensive training courses, might improve the capability of the sales team, but they would still have to fight the impact of the other causes. Taking a 'functional' approach to problem solving can also spawn a large number of improvement projects. This can lead to initiative fatigue.

Third, even if the root causes are correctly identified and addressed, we face an issue if the underlying thinking does not change. The existing thinking and 'the system' slowly strangle the remedy. The new computer system is not used properly because the users were not involved in its design. The strategy is not implemented effectively because managers have not had a voice in it and a clear understanding of it. The required change does not happen because people do not perceive the need for it; there is not enough positive dissatisfaction. We may change the organisation chart, processes and procedures, but unless the thinking changes behaviour will stay the same. If behaviour is the same, nothing has really changed. Existing thinking will thwart the solution.

However, a combination of some short-term improvement, and the need to continue to find another 'cure' for improved performance, leads to the search and purchase of another quick-fix remedy. A further sticking plaster appears on the body of the business, and the underlying thinking of managers and staff may remain, untouched, ready to emasculate the next 'solution'.

The major shift in thinking required is to move to process thinking. Leaders and all people at work need to start to see the organisation as one interdependent system. We have already expressed our views that over a number of decades we have developed a traditional way of thinking about management. Overall this approach was based on a few people having all the information and making all the decisions, and the workers being told what to do. This was born out of the move to mass production techniques in the early part of the twentieth century. The issue is not that this 'command and control' approach was not of value, but that we have perhaps not continued to learn. Perhaps we have not learned to sufficiently question the assumptions that govern the way we run our organisations.

Solutions are created for a problem at a particular point in time. As times change and the forces in that time shift, how safe is it to assume that the problem is the same, or that the thinking that gave us the original solution is still correct?

In short, many of the management practices that we have come to think of as 'normal' were originally developed in response to problems of their time. Today they may be causing damage to our organisations. Similarly, until everyone believes that the purpose of everyone's job is to serve their personal customers and to meet the expectations of shareholders, processes and jobs are unlikely to be as effective as they should be.

There are two shifts of thinking regarding focus that we would like to dwell on. The first is a move to value the importance of accurately defining the effect. The second we have already covered: the need to value the question 'why' far more highly.

1 Accurately defining the effect

Unless we are rigorous here, we may waste time and resources. If the effect is poor attendance and we set off to tackle it with a 'sheep dip' approach, we may waste time and money on areas that do not need it. If we can be very specific, we can be more focused and effective in our use of resources. The process is simple. It involves systematically asking and answering some questions. The results of these questions are then turned into a clear and specific statement.' The systematic questions are as follows:

1.1 *What is* the problem? For example:
    What is wrong?
    What is the fault?
    What is not as expected?
    What variation in quality are we experiencing?
1.2 *Where is* the problem?
    Where is it observed in the process?
    Where is it observed geographically?
1.3 *When is* the problem?
    When was it observed or reported first?
    For how long have the effects/defects been observed?
    Is it continuing?
    When in time (clock or calendar time)?
1.4 *What is not* the problem?
    What is the closest object, person not affected?
    Are some things/people unaffected?
    What other, similar defects are not occurring?
1.5 *Where is not* the problem?
    Are there some similar places where the effects/defects are not observed: in the process? Geographically?
1.6 *When is not* the problem?
    When was the last time it was known to be all right?
    Were there periods when it didn't happen?
    When did it stop?
    For how long?

Having worked through this systematic approach to clarify the nature of the problem, we now need to express it as a clear and concise problem statement. For example, our deduced problem statement might be, 'Absence rates on Mondays and Fridays are at least 7 per cent higher in the Operations Department than in all other departments.' This allows us to clearly and accurately understand and articulate the problem (effects) we are experiencing. We can now focus our time, effort and money more economically on the priority areas. Now that we understand the precise nature of the problem, we can begin to investigate the root causes of it.

2 Deducing the root causes

By asking the question 'why' several times, we are far more likely to explore the nature of the root causes. If we return to the example of the stressed employee, a 'why-based' conversation with this person may help to uncover the root causes of the stress. For instance:

> What do you feel is the main cause of your stress?
> *Too much work and not enough time to do it.*
> Why is that?
> *Because sales promotions from different parts of the business always overlap.*
> Why?
> *Because each part of the business plans its sales campaigns independently.*
> Why is that?
> *Because they all compete against each other and are not encouraged to coordinate their activities.*
> Why do you think that is?
> *I asked the Sales Director that and she said it was her style, the best way she knew to get results.*

So, in this example, the root cause is the Sales Director's chosen leadership style. This in turn creates a fragmented approach which leads to work-flows that are beyond the capacity of the individual. A clear picture of the causes opens a broader range of solutions. The final choice of the solution needs to be considered from a 'whole system' perspective too. The Sales Director might be correct, and the most effective solution for the whole organisation might be to look at using extra temporary people to cover the peaks in workload. Even so, the communication process will need to be improved to allow appropriate planning to take place. One of the most common assumptions regarding problems and results is the tendency to assume that 50 per cent of causes or inputs will account for 50 per cent of results or outputs. This is the road to management hell.

80/20 thinking

> Less is more.
> Robert Browning (1855)

The Italian economist Vilfredo Pareto discovered an imbalance in the distribution of wealth and income in nineteenth century England. He found that the majority of the wealth and income went to a minority of people. In percentage terms 80 per cent of the income and wealth went to 20 per cent of the population.

He found this imbalance repeated consistently when he looked at past records on other countries. The key point is not so much the percentages as the fact that the distribution of wealth is predictably imbalanced. Pareto became known for his 80/20 rule. For example, consider your wardrobe of clothes at home. Chances are that you wear 20 per cent of your clothes for 80 per cent of the time. The percentage split may not be exactly 80/20, but there will be a significant imbalance. This relationship applies everywhere: roughly 80 per cent of the resources are controlled by 20 per cent of the people. Eighty per cent of the sales are made by 20 per cent of the sales staff. About 80 per cent of a company's losses are generated by 20 per cent of the problems, and so on. The 80/20 numbers have stuck as the title, not for reasons of numerical accuracy but to capture the notion of the possibility of significant imbalance.

The 80/20 rule is particularly helpful when applied to problem solving, especially for selecting which problems to address first. You can help your problem solving efforts most by choosing to work on the major problems first: the 20 per cent that provide 80 per cent of the opportunity for improvement. While that may seem obvious, it is not always done. Often people work on problems that are more apparent, more aggravating, or easier to deal with.

The 80/20 principle asserts that 20 per cent of products, customers or employees are really responsible for about 80 per cent of profits. Consequently, the implication is that 80 per cent of products, customers or employees are only contributing some 20 per cent of the profits. This can help us to identify the location of waste.

The 80/20 principle can be applied through general thinking and through specific analysis. As a thinking model, it is used to question where the imbalance might lay. What will provide the biggest return on the resources we are about to use? Who are the critical employees that the organisation depends on? What activities generate the most results? We can apply 80/20 thinking at work and in our daily lives. We can dramatically alter how we use our time and effort by identifying the 20 per cent of time and effort in our lives that is leading to the 80 per cent of value. The scary thing about this level of thinking is that it highlights that a lot of what we do does not contribute to achieving the most important results. It gets even scarier. If we have not used process thinking to clarify the purpose and outputs of what we do, we will be unclear on what is important in the first place! Our potential to waste time, money and resources at work and in our lives is therefore huge. There is never enough time and resources to do everything, but we need to make time to effectively do the important things.

By using specific analysis we can numerically identify the significant imbalances that need to be exploited. We can be far more effective in the use of resources in resolving the problem. If we identify the root causes, and then understand which of the few generate the many, we can target our actions and resources very precisely. We can avoid a 'blanket' approach and use the equivalent of a 'management rifle' rather than a 'shotgun'. For instance, if we track customer complaints and analyse them, we will be able to isolate the minority of issues that cause the majority of complaints. With this clarity we can target our resources to get the best return on our investment.

Root cause analysis and the effective use of the 80/20 principle are practical tools for focus. They provide the insight that illuminates the key drivers of performance. It illuminates what we need to simplify, where we should invest our time, money and effort, and which activities add little value and should be stopped.

Measurement, planning and review

> For man plans, but God arranges.
> Thomas à Kempis (*c.* 1380–1471)

> Nobody ever drew up his plans for life so well but what the facts,
> And the years, and experience always introduce some modifications.
> Terence (160 BC)

Clarifying focus is a critical quality for leadership. However, it loses much of its value if others do not understand what the focus is, and whether success is being achieved. This calls for a systematic approach to identifying what to measure, reviewing in order to learn from the measures, and using this to plan improvement. The process should be a continuous cycle.

Measurement has to be the start point, but what we measure, and why and what we do with this information, make the difference. Most managers recognise the value of measuring things. 'What gets

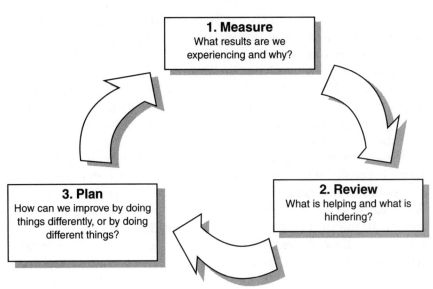

Figure 4.2

measured gets done' is a simple but powerful management reminder. If you agree with the statement, then it follows that if we measure the wrong things, or use them the wrong way, we can easily do more harm than good.

In 1086 William I was responsible for initiating a massive measurement exercise, the Domesday Survey, which eventually was set out in what we know now as the *Domesday Book* (in the eleventh century it was known as 'the description' or 'the boke of Winchester'). The survey was an incredibly impressive and considerable undertaking, measuring the wealth and income of (most of) England and, therefore, importantly how much tax revenue William could raise. For most governments, maximising such revenues is at the forefront of their minds, but for William I the continual battles and rebellions and the need to raise monies to fund armies provided a particularly urgent need. In the 1,700 pages of the *Domesday Book*, 13,418 different places in England were described in considerable detail, including the amount and type of land held and by whom; the number of mills and churches; even the number and value of livestock.

The efficiency and speed of the survey are to be admired even today, but unfortunately for William he instigated the work a little too late in his reign to achieve significant benefit, because he died a year or so after the survey was completed. Despite not benefiting personally from the

Domesday survey, when he commissioned it William knew exactly what would be done with the information gained, because for the remaining year of his reign he was able to raise greater taxes (based on a more logical and measurement-based process).

It is reasonably clear that William I realised where the buck stopped: with him. On his deathbed he allegedly expressed his accountability in the following statement: 'I persecuted the native inhabitants of England beyond all reason. Whether nobles or commons, I cruelly oppressed them; many I unjustly disinherited; innumerable multitudes, especially in the county of York, perished through me by famine and sword. I am stained with the tears of blood that I have shed.' It is unclear whether in making the statement he was setting the record straight in this life or clearing the decks for the next.

Some traditional approaches to measuring corporate performance have been quite narrow. The focus is often aimed at measuring financial outcomes. Whilst this is a critical measure for any business, it does not tell us anything about how these results were achieved. If we are unclear about the reasons for success or failure, it is difficult to reproduce success and initiate improvement. Surely it is as important to be measuring the key drivers that lead to the achievement of these financial results. For instance, measuring cost or productivity but not measuring the specific things that customers value can easily lead us to cut out things that deliver customer satisfaction and repeat business. For example, measuring call times in a call centre encourages people to be fast, but not necessarily accurate or service-focused, so we run the risk of 'making the numbers' on call times, but at the cost of customer service or accuracy. Both could be huge costs to the organisation. The first might drastically reduce the lifetime value of customers, reducing future profits. The second might lead to mistakes and rework, increasing costs. Clearly, managing costs and achieving profit are important dimensions of performance, but they measure 'whats' rather than 'hows' and 'whys'. We need a balanced set of measures that reflect the drivers of financial success. We observe a number of characteristics that are associated with the 'traditional' approach to measurement.

- The measures mainly focus on what has happened. There is little energy used to understand why it happened and how to improve it in the future.
- Measures are too narrow and tend to measure outputs ('whats'), which are predominantly financially driven.

82

- There is an over-emphasis on measuring costs.
- There are too many measures to be truly useful.
- There is little focused action around the information.
- Poor reporting processes render the measures ineffective for real time decision making. By the time the output measure is published it is usually too late to correct things. This is wasteful and frustrating.
- Feedback is often 'hidden' in managers' offices. This drains the motivation of the people doing the job, as they are unclear whether they are making a difference. It also 'sucks up' the decision making to managers, as the rest of the team do not have valid information to decide from or act on. Equally, it is difficult to use your initiative if you do not perceive the need to improve anything!

If we applied this logic to driving a car it might look something like this.

- Drive by predominantly looking in the rearview mirror.
- Install at least 50 instruments on the dashboard.
- Do not allow the driver to see these instruments. They are very complex and need interpreting by a more experienced person in the passenger seat.
- Instruct the passenger to look through the windscreen and periodically lean across to inspect the dashboard.
- The passenger should then decide what information to pass on to the driver, when he or she has interpreted it all.

Clearly this would be ineffective. The driver would fail to learn and adapt in time to improve performance, or even keep the car on the road! If the car ran into something, the driver would know something was wrong but would still have to wait for the passenger to explain what had happened and what to do next. Anyone recommending such an approach to driving would probably be regarded as mad. Yet we believe similar thinking is alive and well in many organisations. The focus is mainly in the past, and the information appears to be used to apportion blame and hand out direct or indirect 'punishment'. Such an approach is likely to encourage a culture where:

- more energy goes into avoiding the blame than solving the problem
- initiative is seen as a risky business, and is avoided
- the same problems occur with regular monotony.

This kind of environment is in direct contrast to the fast, fluid and competitive market in which most organisations operate. To change this, we again need to start with a shift in thinking. At the heart of this shift is the thought that the purpose of measurement is to learn why things have happened so we can reduce:

- variation
- time taken
- cost
- wastage
- re-work
- stress.

In turn, this will promote improved quality through consistency, and improved profit through productivity.

We recommend the following principles for using measurement to better effect.

- *Measurement should be encouraged to promote learning and improvement.* Value not just the 'what' but also the 'why'. If performance improves, find out why so it can be repeated. If performance falls, find out why so it can be improved.
- *Identify the **vital few** 'output' measures.* These should be deduced from what really matters to customers and shareholders.
- *Identify the critical control points for each of the vital few output measures.* These are the points that make or break a process. (For instance, when making a cup of tea, having the water at boiling point is a critical point. Pouring under-heated water onto the tea just creates waste and re-work.)
- *Develop simple measurement processes at the control points.* Make these available 'real time' to the people who do the job. These are the 'early warning systems' that shout at us to take action. If we do not, the output measures will not be achieved and productivity and quality will suffer.
- *Give the people doing the job the responsibility and authority to act on the information the measures provide.* They are the closest to the action. Train them and allow them to collect, interpret and act on the data to keep the process on track.
- *Encourage people to use their initiative to drive improvement.* Recognise their efforts, even when they do not work out.

- *Take a firm line with those who don't act on what the information tells them* and those who repeatedly make the same mistakes.

Review

Effective review is a vital component of focus. It is the source of positive dissatisfaction and the root of continuous improvement. Without pausing to review how and why things are going the way they are, we run the risk of becoming complacent, stagnant and locked in a cycle of waste and repeated mistakes. We often hear people say things like, 'I have got 15 years' experience in this business.' Is this true, or is it one year's experience repeated 14 times? While learning is a natural condition, effective learning needs effort. This is even more the case when we want to stimulate group/team learning. Can you imagine a professional football team not training together? Can you picture them not reviewing their learning together? Those who need to work together, need to learn together.

The pressures of modern life often encourage us to move from one item on the 'To Do' list to another, at an increasing pace. The temptation therefore is to not leave enough space for learning and improvement through review. How many of your meetings finish with a ten-minute discussion of what went well in the process of the meeting? Do you agree one or two points that the team should work on next time in order to improve the effectiveness of the meeting? If you do, congratulations. Our experience is that you are in a minority. If you do not, how are your meetings likely to improve?

As with everything in life, our results are helped by following an effective process. The purpose of this process is to produce insight into the causes and effects of our decisions and actions. The process can also be used to facilitate learning from unplanned events. The key steps involve identifying what happened, understanding why it happened and what can be learned from the experience. The final step, creating a plan of what to do differently next time, is crucial if the learning is to be translated into improvement. The cycle continues and in effect becomes a 'corkscrew' of continuous improvement.

The following suggestions are offered for getting the most out of this process.

- Initiate the process immediately after the events you wish to analyse have taken place. Feelings and emotions associated with an experience are easier to capture while they are fresh in our memory.
- When reviewing the experience, work hard at avoiding blame. The

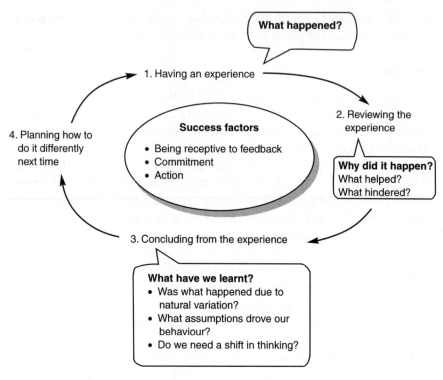

Figure 4.3
Source: based on the work of Kolb

review is about understanding what happened, why, and how to improve. Apportioning blame in public kills honesty and open discussion. Furthermore, learning is impeded, as individuals do not want to contribute to the discussions and accept accountability for fear of blame and punishment. Using the questions 'What helped?' and 'What hindered?' and recording the views of the team on a flipchart helps to focus on learning rather than victimisation.

- During the 'concluding from the experience' step, identify those outcomes that can be directly attributed to the action that was taken. (It may be necessary to take into account key external and historical factors that may have influenced the outcome.) Emotions and attitudes as well as substantive results should be identified at this step. Which behaviours, emotions and assumptions had the most significant influence on the outcomes?
- During the 'concluding from the experience' step, make connections between the 'whats' and 'whys' of the experience. Use

these insights to develop new theories, hypotheses, principles or guidelines, or to improve old ones.

- Document your learning and conclusions as well as the Action Plan so they can be shared with others and be used to guide future actions and decisions.

- People need to value feedback as constructive and essential to improvement, rather than seeing it as a threat and engaging in defensive behaviour. This needs to be encouraged by leading through example.

- The learning will only translate into improvement if the Action Plan is implemented. Participants therefore need to be committed to the plan, and express this commitment through action. Actions should be reviewed regularly. If progress is not being made, this should become the subject of a review discussion. It is vital to challenge non-completion of actions to which individuals have committed. If we do not, then complacency easily creeps in. By definition, if someone truly commits to something, they will do it. If there are genuine unanticipated events, then allowances need to be made. If someone is treating commitment lightly, it needs to be addressed.

When groups follow this process, analysis of what happened and why it happened proceeds at a reasonably fast pace. When the analysis is drawn out, interest and energy will drop, which results in a reduction of value and impact.

Planning

Planning is about more than creating an action plan. It is concerned with clarifying responsibility and generating ownership. People own what they help to create. It is difficult to feel part of something that you do not understand. Equally, why should people feel committed to a plan if they have not had a voice in shaping it? All too often plans fail because people do not understand the need for the plan, or the logic behind it. If we want people to be committed to action, we need to involve them in the planning. Planning should be a collective activity which generates mutual understanding. If individuals have been involved in the measurement and review steps of the process, mutual understanding of the issue and its causes will already be high.

Much has been written about how to plan. It is a huge management topic in its own right. However, in the spirit of process thinking and simplification, we believe the essence of the process is as follows.

1. Assemble the people essential to a successful implementation.
2. Clarify the purpose of doing it.
3. Specify the particular outputs that must be delivered.
4. Agree/specify the completion date (and any other critical dates en route to the completion date).
5. Generate a list of all the steps that need to be taken.
6. Analyse the steps for any dependencies (that is, which steps cannot be completed until another is in place).
7. Identify which activities can run in parallel.
8. Put the steps into their logical sequence.
9. Deduce the completion date necessary for each step by starting at the completion date and working backwards. (For example, if the completion date is to arrive at Harrods in London on 24 December, what time do we need to arrive at the nearest underground station? What time do we need to arrive at Heathrow Airport in order to get to that underground station on time? Therefore what flight must we take to get us to Heathrow on time? And so on.)
10. Agree a specific individual who will accept responsibility for delivering each step by the due date.
11. Agree key review dates to monitor progress.
12. Document the plan and make sure everyone has a copy.

Most of all, we urge you to remember that the objective of a plan is to get things done. There are no prizes for having the best plan. The plan should suit the task. The important thing is to have a plan to focus the efficient use of time, talent and resources in order to achieve a result. We should not even expect the plan to be the same. The world around us is continually changing. Frustrating as it may be, it is our job to change our plans in the light of these shifting circumstances. If you really want to make God laugh, show him your (fixed) plans!

 ## Focus: key points

- There is never enough time or resources to do everything. The effective individual works out what is important and focuses on it relentlessly.
- Complexity is inefficient. It wastes time, materials and mental energy and causes stress, anxiety frustration and disillusionment.

- Complexity creeps up on us. As things evolve, they are adapted and bastardised, becoming more complex. Those who grow up with this get used to the complexity and no longer notice it.
- As leaders, we need to value simplicity and encourage this value in our colleagues. We need to challenge complexity, and challenge people to find simpler ways to get work done.
- Prior to simplifying something we need to fully understand how a process works before we mess with it. If we act without understanding, we run the risk of being simpletons.
- The process we follow always heavily influences the results we experience. If we want a different result, we need to do things differently, or do different things.
- Process thinking is the very heart of effective leadership and management.
- Asking 'why' encourages us to focus on being effective.
- Asking 'how' prompts us to challenge the process, to find the simplest and most efficient way of achieving the required result.
- A clear and mutual understanding of purpose is critical to individual and organisation success.
- Outputs need to be deduced from the purpose.
- Where possible, output measures should reflect a balance of requirements such as quantity, quality, time, cost and behaviour.
- Having clarified the 'why' and the 'what' we can now move on to the 'how' (process). How do we need to organise and work in order to deliver the 'what' with minimum stress and resources?
- Unless we search out and understand root causes, we have not focused on solving the problem, just the manifestation of the problem.
- It is our view that many improvement initiatives fail because:
  - the causes of the performance problem are not identified and understood
  - the problem and the solution are treated in

isolation, rather than as part of a complex and interdependent system
- the underlying thinking does not change.
- Leaders and all people at work need to start to see the organisation as one interdependent system.
- Many of the management practices that we have come to think of as 'normal' were originally developed in response to problems of their time. Today they may be causing damage to our organisations.
- By understanding the precise nature of the problem, we can focus our time, effort and money more economically on the priority areas.
- By asking the question 'why' several times, we are far more likely to explore the nature of the root causes.
- The Pareto principle shows that there is significant imbalance between causes and effects, effort and results. A key few things generate the majority of the result.
- If we identify the root causes, and then understand which of the few generate the many, we can target our actions and resources very precisely.
- With this clarity we can target our resources to get the best return on our investment.
- Traditional approaches to measuring corporate performance have been quite narrow. The focus is often aimed at measuring financial outcomes.
- We need a balanced set of measures that reflect the drivers of success.
- The traditional approach to measures tends to focus mainly in the past, and the information appears to be used to apportion blame and hand out direct or indirect 'punishment'.
- The purpose of measurement is to *learn why* things have happened so we can reduce:
  - variation
  - time taken
  - cost
  - wastage
  - re-work
  - stress.

- Measurement should be used to promote learning and improvement.
- Identify the *vital few* 'output' measures.
- Identify the critical control points for each of the vital few output measures.
- Develop simple measurement processes at the control points.
- Give the people doing the job the responsibility and authority to act on the information the measures provide.
- Encourage people to use their initiative to drive improvement.
- Take a firm line with those who do not act on what the information tells them and those who repeatedly make the same mistakes.
- Effective review is a vital component of focus. It is the source of positive dissatisfaction and the root of continuous improvement.
- Initiate the review process immediately after the events you wish to analyse have taken place.
- When reviewing the experience work hard at avoiding blame.
- Planning is about more than creating an action plan. It is concerned with clarifying responsibility and generating ownership.
- People own what they help to create.
- There are no prizes for having the best plan. The plan should suit the task.

Focus toolbox

As you will hopefully have concluded by now, our belief is that change and improvement in others must first start with change and improvement in us. Without this, we are not in a position to lead by example. The following questions help to improve focus. If you choose to make a habit of them you will experience improvement in your focus. If you use them with other people, listen to their answers and support them to act, you will encourage focus as a way of life in your team or organisation.

- Why are we doing/do we want to do this, and for whom?

- What specific outputs (results) are we aiming to achieve and for whom?
- How does it contribute to the achievement of our/your purpose and outputs?
- Is this valued by customers?
- Is this valued by our shareholders/trustees?
- Is this valued by our employees?
- Why are we doing this?

- Why do we do it this way?
- How did it come to be done this way?
- Do we really need to continue to do it this way? Why?

- Why do we need to do this?
- What would happen if we stopped doing it? Why?
- What other ways are there to do it?

- Where do we experience problems? Why?
- Where are things too complicated? Why?
- What are the root causes that create most of the problems? Why?
- What causes us waste? Why?
- What slows things down? Why?
- What causes you frustration and stress? Why?

- How can we simplify things with no loss in output, productivity, quality and service?
- How can we reduce waste with no loss in output, productivity, quality and service?
- How can we reduce the time it takes with no loss in output, productivity, quality and service?
- How can we remove frustration and stress with no loss in output, productivity, quality and service?

- If we were starting from scratch, how would you want to do it? Why?

Timeless Management historical illustrations

Timeless Manager 5: Prince Albert – focus

Prince Albert (1819–1861). Prince Consort of Queen Victoria of Great Britain.

Connections with Historic Royal Palaces

Prince Albert and Queen Victoria first met a year before she acceded to the throne, at her childhood home of Kensington Palace. Victoria lived here with her mother, the Duchess of Kent, until she became Queen, and Albert made a brief visit. The impression he made on Victoria on this occasion was to last; as she wrote a day or two later 'he possesses every quality that could be desired to render me perfectly happy'.

After their marriage, Victoria and Albert did not live at any of the Historic Royal Palaces, but Prince Albert was very influential in the way they were treated in the nineteenth century. He promoted plans to restore the buildings of the Tower to their medieval appearance, taking a close interest in the restoration of the Salt Tower in the 1850s. On his advice the top floor of the White Tower was opened to the public in the 1860s: it would otherwise have continued to be treated as a military warehouse rather than a historic building.

Historical illustration

When the 20-year-old Francis Albert Augustus Charles Emmanuel, Prince of Saxe-Coburg-Gotha arrived in England in 1840 to marry his cousin he brought with him an unhappy childhood, a strong German accent, a fine intellect and, among other qualities, the timeless trait of 'focus'.

The application of this trait was probably necessary on a personal level to convert the arranged marriage to Queen Victoria into a highly successful, enduring, although perhaps emotionally one-sided, relationship. Undoubtedly the Queen fell passionately in love with Albert, but arguably this was not reciprocated, his feelings being more of affection and gratitude than love.

However, the focus trait was inappropriate and inconvenient for his prime early role as husband of the Queen. In this role Prince Albert was supposed to be the passive companion and escort to the monarch of the greatest empire on the planet. Such a world power did not need or require its Queen's spouse to use his intelligence or ability or express his own opinions in public. It was not that Albert did not know what was expected of him – he just did not accept it. Even before his marriage he wrote to his grandmother that he intended to be 'untiring in my efforts and labours for the country to which I shall in future belong'.

During the next 22 years until his death from typhoid in 1861, Albert applied all of his talents and focus in masterly, determined and sometimes subtle ways, and in doing so he made significant, long-lasting contributions to the educational, artistic, political and scientific life of his adopted country. He threw himself wholeheartedly, just as he promised his grandmother, into a wide range of jobs, from his early chairmanship of the Royal Commission to select works of art for the (new) Palace of Westminster to more substantial roles as Chancellor of Cambridge University, President of the Society of Arts, Master of Trinity House and, importantly, the Queen's Private Secretary and adviser. He helped to found the Royal College of Chemistry, acquired and developed the royal properties at Osborne House and Balmoral Castle, reorganised the Royal Household, and of course he was key to the success of the Great Exhibition in 1851.

The bold way in which the Prince tackled the reorganisation of the Royal Household in 1844 is a classic example of the use of the focus trait and one of its subsets: simplicity. The reorganisation required meticulous planning, thorough analysis of the problem and persistence and perseverance to force through the desired changes. Two relatively minor but persistent problems illustrated that all was not well within the Household: the windows of Buckingham Palace were not always clean, and the Palace fires not lit!

The main reason for these inconveniences was a confused and confusing organisation structure. Cleaning the inside of the windows was the responsibility of two very senior and equally independent Household heads, the Lord Chamberlain or the Lord Steward, and the outside of the windows was cleaned by the Office of Woods and Forests. Similarly, the Lord Steward had ultimate responsibility for preparing the fires and the Lord Chamberlain for lighting them. There was little coordination between the various departments: for example the windows would be cleaned on the inside but not on the outside, and vice versa. Similarly, kindling would be laid for the fires when there was no one to light them, and the staff would turn up with their matches to find no kindling.

The inefficiency of the Palace manifested itself in other more serious ways. A persistent 17-year-old intruder, dubbed 'the boy Jones' by the newspapers of the time, breached Palace security on at least three occasions, once allegedly for a period of three days. Thankfully, he seemed to have no ill will towards the Royal family, just a weird fascination which is still not really understood.

The profligacy of the Household was also uncovered by Albert: for example the payment of 35 shillings a week to officers of the guard whose duties had long since finished. The payment to the phantom officers had instead been made to an under butler.

These inefficiencies and abuses of the system were swept away by Albert's complete reorganisation of the Household. Despite determined opposition to his reforms, Albert succeeded in unifying the operations under a single head – the Master of the Household – who assumed responsibility for all the palaces. A confusing and complicated structure had been replaced by a simple and workable one. The changes led initially to complaints and accusations of unnecessary interference but, in due course, the leaner and more efficient Royal Household became a respected organisation, and with it Albert's reputation was also enhanced.

Albert's endurance and ability were to be tested much more by his management of the Great Exhibition of 1851. Apart from focus it required meticulous planning, a focus trait subset. In its initial stages this major enterprise bore remarkable similarities to the Millennium Dome: the Crystal Palace was also a large and unusual structure (it was 1,848 ft long and 408 ft wide, one of the great engineering achievements of the century); lack of financial resource; political and religious opponents; press and public opposition to the cost and scale of the structure; and the controversial location in Hyde Park. It was hard to find a supporter and it was widely forecast to be a failure.

For the whole of the two-year development phase Albert wrestled with these problems with amazing energy and overcame them, at some cost to his health. His efforts were rewarded because, unlike the Dome, the Great Exhibition was a stunning success and received international acclaim, mainly because of Albert's drive but also perhaps partly because of the strength and appeal of its theme, 'Industry of all Nations'. The more local critics were converted almost overnight to supporters, and the 'palace of glass' was visited by 6 million people (a much higher proportion of the population than visited the Dome) in just six months. Not only was the Great Exhibition self-financing, despite not charging exhibitors to pay to exhibit, but it actually made a profit of £165,000. This profit was eventually used to acquire 87 acres of land in South Kensington where a collection of museums (including the Victoria & Albert Museum), colleges and art venues were eventually built. This complex remains today as a legacy of the German prince.

Despite the success of the Great Exhibition and his important contributions and service to Great Britain, during his lifetime Albert was never fully accepted by its people. History will tell a different story and will judge him as the most successful royal partner of all time, contributing more than many monarchs, an uncrowned king and a brilliant exponent of Timeless Management.

Timeless Manager 6: Sir Isaac Newton – process thinking, causes and measurement

Sir Isaac Newton (1642–1727), physicist and mathematician. Professor of Mathematics (Cambridge University), Member of Parliament and President of the Royal Society.

Connections with Historic Royal Palaces

Before the Royal Mint moved into a purpose-built building in 1810, the coinage of the realm was minted within the walls of the Tower of London. Isaac Newton presided over the organisation, as Master of the Mint from 1699 until 1727. He had offices at the Tower of London, and as chief officer of the Mint worked hard to prosecute counterfeiters and improve the working of the institution.

The Mint had always to compete for space and privileges in the Tower with the other departments based there, and Newton fiercely protected the Mint and its authority against the Lieutenant of the Tower and the Master of the Ordnance.

Historical illustration

At his birth in 1642 he was very small and weak, and it was touch and go whether Isaac Newton would survive his first day. In the next 85 years until his death in 1727, his effect on the development of modern science was profound: he was, simply, its most important contributor. Alexander Pope described this contribution most succinctly:

> Nature and Natures Laws lay hid in night,
> God said, let Newton be! And all was light.

Initially at school in Grantham his reports described him as 'inattentive' and 'idle'. This attitude may have been caused by an unhappy childhood. His father died shortly before his birth, and his mother remarried Barnabas Smith, Minister of the local church. When at age

19 he looked back on his sins he included 'threatening my father and mother Smith to burn them and their house over them'. No wonder they promptly farmed him out to live with his grandmother.

Following the death of his hated stepfather and an unsuccessful period out of school managing his mother's interests and property, Newton returned to Grantham School. Whether it was through the tutelage of Stokes, the school's headmaster (with whom he lodged) or the encouragement of William Ayscough, his uncle, his approach changed and he developed a hunger for learning. In 1661 Newton began his studies at Cambridge University. He became first Fellow of Trinity College then Lucasian Professor.

As a genius physicist and mathematician, Newton was a great process thinker. He is renowned for developing simple analytical ways that draw together a number of different and apparently unrelated problem solving methods. In his book *Principia*, arguably the greatest book ever written on science, he described a new process for scientific reasoning. The process was set out as four rules, which at the time were groundbreaking:

1. We are to admit no more causes of natural things such as are both true and sufficient to explain their appearances.
2. The same natural effects must be assigned to the same causes.
3. Qualities of bodies are to be esteemed as universal.
4. Propositions deduced from observation of phenomena should be viewed as accurate until other phenomena contradict them.

In his later book *Opticks* he developed this process thinking further:

As in mathematics, so in natural philosophy the investigation of difficult things by the method of analysis ought ever to precede the method of composition. This analysis consists of making experiments and observations, and in drawing general conclusions from them by induction ... by this way of analysis we may proceed from compounds to ingredients, and from motions to the forces producing them; and in general from effects to their causes, and from particular causes to more general ones till the argument end in the most general. This is the method of analysis: and the synthesis consists in assuming the causes discovered and established as principles, and by them explaining the phenomena proceeding from them, and proving the explanations.

As to causes, he studied the nature of light and concluded that white light was caused by a mixture of colours which can be separated by refraction. His second great work *Opticks* set out the new theory of matter, and this led to experiments into heat, light magnetism and eventually electricity.

In 1672 Newton wrote about his method of determining causes through a flexible approach to experimentation: 'The way therefore to examine it is by considering whether the experiments which I propound do prove those parts of the theory to which they are applied, or by prosecuting other experiments which the theory may suggest for its examination.'

In undertaking his revolutionary scientific work Newton would never challenge or conflict the religious beliefs of the age. His view was set out clearly in a letter to Edmund Halley in 1686: 'Does it not appear from phenomena that there is a Being incorporeal, living, intelligent, omnipresent, who in infinite space, as it were in his sensory, sees the things themselves intimately and thoroughly perceives them, and comprehends them wholly?'

In public at least, he personified humility. He is quoted as saying, 'I don't know what I may seem to the world, but as to myself, I seem to have been only like a boy playing on the sea shore, and diverting myself in now and then finding a smoother pebble or prettier shell than ordinary, whilst the great ocean of truth lay all undiscovered before me.'

Obviously measurement was key to Newton's work as a scientist, as was his use of mathematics in the solving of scientific problems. His interest in mathematics was spawned in 1663 when he purchased a book on astrology at a fair in Cambridge and discovered that he could not understand the mathematics in it. He then studied trigonometry, geometry and algebra. During the closure of Cambridge University due to the plague in 1665 he worked from home in Lincolnshire. There, effectively, he laid the basis for differential and integral calculus.

Rather than take it easy at 57, a grand old age for the period, he became Master of the Royal Mint then located at the Tower of London. He applied his scientific reasoning and process thinking to prevent counterfeiting of the coinage and to a difficult re-coinage operation. He displayed incredible energy when he first took on this role – a complete change from academia – and often turned up at 4 am, the time the coin presses started to operate. He turned his intellect and his process thinking capability to the task of making the operation of the Royal Mint more efficient by undertaking a very detailed process review. Effectively, this work was the forerunner to time and motion study. He recorded his observations:

> Two mills with 4 millers, 12 horses, two horse keepers, 3 cutters, 2 flatters, 8 sizers, one nealer, three blanchers, two markers, two presses with 14 labourers to pull at them can coin after the rate of a thousand weight or 3000 lib (pounds) of money per diem.

Newton increased the production by ensuring proper coordination between the motion of the press and the action of the coiner, so that the conversion time from blank to pressed coin could be increased to between 50 and 55 a minute.

As the greatest scientist who has ever lived was a humble man, he would certainly not have approved of the inscription on his tomb in Westminster Abbey 'Mortals! rejoice at so great an ornament to the human race'. He would have been wrong.

5 Clarity

A matter that becomes clear ceases to concern us.
Nietzsche, 1886

Have something to say, and say it as clearly as you can.
That is the only secret of style.
Matthew Arnold (1822–1888)

Much effort is wasted due to a lack of clarity. Focus helps us to identify what is important. To pursue it effectively and efficiently we need to be able to align people's roles and skills on the right things. Without this, committed people will do the wrong things right. A critical leadership skill is the ability to provide clarity on what is expected. We believe the key components here are:

- communication
- expectations
- responsibility
- allowing and delegating.

Communication

To think justly, we must understand what others mean: to know the value of our thoughts, we must try their effect on other minds.
William Hazlitt, 1826

When the eyes say one thing and the tongue another, a practised man relies on the language of the first.

Emerson, 1860

Communication has been a concern for every organisation we have worked in. In many ways it is the elusive golden prize. An enormous amount of time and literature has been generated in this area, and rightly so. Effective communication is the lifeblood of any relationship.

101

As relationships are central to personal and organisational success, it is truly a critical component of high performance. When you ask people, 'What holds you back from achieving more in your job?' or 'What are the major sources of frustration in this organisation?', communication gets repeat billings. Leaders may be exercising many hours in figuring out how to put a communication system together that will improve things. This is important, but it is only part of the story.

Queen Elizabeth I was an ace communicator. She believed it necessary to communicate with her people and used ways of doing this which predated the modern spin doctor. From the start of her reign, at the eve of her coronation procession, not only did she use this event to interact with the thousands who attended but she actually employed a reporter to record her remarks. After a procession a leaflet was published entitled *The Queen Majesty's Passing Through the City of London to Westminster*. Not only would Alastair Campbell, Tony Blair's chief spin doctor, have wanted to instigate this coverage, he would have been proud of the Queen's management of the procession:

- The litter which carried her was open on every side so that she could be seen by the people.
- She kept a sprig of rosemary given to her by a poor woman all the way to Westminster.
- All along the route Elizabeth stopped, listened and replied sensitively to good wishes.
- The five pageants or set pieces staged on the route, which historically had been one-way events, elicited real responses from Elizabeth, to the delight of the crowds.

The new Queen was image-conscious and throughout her reign understood the need to communicate with her people. She saw this as being critical, as a woman, to retaining the throne. She introduced a number of colourful events, for example the Accession Day tilts which were held annually to celebrate the Queen ascending the throne. There were also a number of well publicised royal progresses undertaken throughout Southern England, when the Queen visited the important population centres with the aim of projecting a favourable image by establishing direct contact with her people.

As with her first public events, the Queen used the progresses as two-way communication exercises: she stopped to talk to people, she listened. But she did not just rely on royal progresses to practise her communication skills. Her speech to her soldiers at the encampment at Tilbury at the time of the battle with the Spanish Armada was nothing less than inspirational:

> I am come amongst you.... Resolved in the midst of battle to live or die amongst you all. To lay down for God and for my kingdom and for my people my honour my blood even in the dust. I know I have the body of a weak and feeble woman but I have the heart and stomach of a King, and a King of England, too.

Elizabeth's great oratorical skills were also used when she gave her last dignified speech to parliament: 'And thou God hath raised me high, yet this I count the glory of my Crown, that I have reigned with your loves.' Not only did she win the nation's heart during her reign, but in a December 2001 poll of BBC Radio's *Today* programme listeners, just 400 years after her death, she was voted Britain's greatest-ever monarch. This undoubtedly was due in large measure to her achievements while in power, but interestingly, some credit has been given to a recent film (*Elizabeth*, starring Cate Blanchett) and the Starkey television series. No doubt this communication success would have given her great satisfaction. But how can such successes be achieved in today's organisation?

We believe, as ever, that the place to start is with the individual. Unless managers and employees accept their responsibility for effective communication, the systems become management-driven and wither on the vine. For people to accept responsibility for communication they usually need help with two things: a shift in thinking, and the skills to communicate effectively. We will begin to explore both of these by putting forward and explaining our views on some fundamental principles for effective communication. None of us are perfect, and communication is an area that is guaranteed to remind us of this fact. However, we suggest the following principles as a route map to reduce the frequency of our communication glitches.

Ten timeless principles for effective communication

1. Listen to understand.
2. Reach mutual understanding before anything is done.
3. Focus on finding solutions together, not winning.
4. Think straight and talk straight, in that order.

5.   Say it in 30 seconds or less.
6.   Start with the big picture.
7.   Use the right medium.
8.   Go at their pace.
9.   Use their language.
10. Summarise and test for understanding.

Listen to understand

It is not the speaker who controls communication but the listener.

Anon.

Here is a quick question for you. What is the difference between data, information and communication? Our view is that data is a collection of facts or opinions. Information comes about when the data is organised and analysed to the point where it offers insight or learning. However, communication does not take place until all parties involved understand the information. They 'perceive the same picture'. The essence of effective communication is mutual understanding.

Using our definitions, our experience is that many organisations are data rich and communication poor. Unless people internalise the information into 'So what this means for me is ...' , we are unlikely to have communicated. Equally, we are unlikely to see any action from that person.

Achieving mutual understanding needs a communications partnership. Speakers need to be clear and concise in their expression. Recipients need to listen to understand. Consequently, a vital part of listening to understand is to ask questions for absolute clarity. It is at these two points that the responsibility for communication is often abrogated. The speaker does not sufficiently engage brain and express the ideas in a user-friendly manner, and the recipient loses concentration and does not ask questions. We can draw from history a lesson of what happened when there was a breakdown between send and receive. In October 1854 at the Battle of Balaclava, Lord Raglan the commanding officer (who was not at the scene) issued an order to stop guns being carried away during their retreat. This order was misinterpreted that the Light Brigade under the command of Lord Cardigan should charge the Russian artillery. This they did with massive loss of life in the Charge of the Light Brigade.

There are several different levels of listening. At the two extremes we have barely listening at all, and what we call 'generous listening'. Barely listening is characterised by those moments when your ears are working but your brain is engaged on something else: for example, watching something interesting on television when your partner is speaking to you. You are aware that there is another noise in the room, you even know who is making it, and vaguely what the subject matter is, but you are focused elsewhere. This is a surefire way of triggering a reaction in your partner. The message he or she perceives is often along the lines of 'You are more interested in that than me, so it must be more important to you than I am.'

Listening to people is a mark of respect. It signals to them that we value them enough to choose to give them our attention. The opposite is also true. If people feel that you do not listen to them, it puts distance and strain into the relationship. It can reduce their commitment. 'Why should I be interested in helping you when you are not interested in me?'

This is a non-work example, but challenge yourself to think about how you listen at work. How many times are you distracted by pressing deadlines? How about a previous conversation that did not go well? Then there is the telephone, or the arriving email perhaps. Oh yes, and that new memo you have just noticed on your desk. Perhaps even the distraction of a passing aesthetically pleasing colleague? There are two key points here. The first is that effective listening requires us to listen with our minds. We have to be fully focused in our head as well as our ears. The second is that effective listening is an act of generosity. It is concerned with quietening your mind to attend only to what the other person is saying to you. When we are focused on people and their point of view, when we are seeking only to understand their views, and how they feel, this is the highest level of listening. We are not judging, or disagreeing, we are just working hard to understand how they perceive and feel about the situation. We are seeking to listen with empathy, to perceive things as they do. This is a great skill. It helps to build strong relationships. People feel that you value them. They know that you are interested in understanding their views before you state your own. It is a mark of respect. By exploring each other's perceptions of the situation we can reach mutual understanding. We may still disagree, but we understand why we disagree. Both parties feel that they are entitled to their point of view, whatever the final decision or outcome. We do not feel belittled. Contrast this with ineffective listening. Often people are merely pausing for mental breath before their next interruption. If you observe conversations and meetings, there is a frighteningly high level of poor listening. The predominant principle is often that of being heard.

We are not suggesting that effective listening is easy. The opposite is true. There is a huge difference between just hearing what people say and making a real effort to understand what they are saying. At a seminar run by John, one of the participants admitted, 'I had always believed I was a good listener, but I understand now that I have only been watching other people's mouths, waiting for them to stop so that I could talk.' Active, empathic listening is a skill which can be developed. However, it requires a great deal of concentration, energy and self-discipline. So what benefits might we gain if we make the effort?

- We learn more.
- People contribute more – because you have shown that you respect their opinions and because there is less chance of their ideas being lost.
- Less time wasted through cross-talk – people wait for others to finish before they come in.
- Increased chance of finding faster solutions, as the emphasis is on finding common ground rather than winning the point.
- Improved quality of solutions, because all members have the opportunity to contribute and explore options.
- More effective meetings. People sometimes fear that active listening will lead to even longer meetings. Interestingly, this does not tend to be the case. Time is saved as people do not feel the need to keep re-introducing the point that no one listened to the first time around.
- Improved ownership of decisions, as those concerned feel they have all had a hand in creating them.

Developing our active listening skills is a lifelong process. The following guidelines, if practised, will lead to a significant improvement in the quality of your listening. They will also lead to a change in the nature of your relationships.

Some more guidelines on how to develop your empathic listening skills are included in the 'Toolbox' section of this chapter.

Reach mutual understanding before anything is done and focus on finding solutions together, not winning

If we apply our active listening skills we can quickly reach a point when we understand the other person's point of view. By having the courtesy to listen to understand, we tend to foster a climate that allows people to explain their perceptions. The focus here is not to prove the other person wrong, or to solve the problem. The aim is purely to understand each other's perspective. By doing so we can gauge how large the gap is between our perceptions of the situation. By asking other people why they perceive things the way they do, and disclosing why we see them the way we do, we can learn about the root causes of our different interpretations. Such an approach builds an environment of trust and cooperation. As such, we are more likely to avoid fighting to make sure our opinion prevails. Instead, we focus on finding the most appropriate solution.

Think straight and talk straight, in that order

If we are unclear about the message we need to convey, the recipient has no hope! Clarifying our thinking before we speak is our prime responsibility as a communicator.

Some people appear to pride themselves in their bluntness or 'shooting from the hip'. We wholeheartedly support being who we are, and no more and no less, in our behaviour. However, the art of effective communication needs us to think like a supplier. If we are driven by our needs, we communicate to suit our purpose. So if we are in a rush, we will speak quickly, often as we are halfway out of the door. If the recipient misunderstands, our instinctive reaction may be that he or she is dim, or, 'Do I have to do everything myself?' We already know what we know. Our purpose is to assist our recipients to understand it as clearly as we do. We therefore need to tailor our delivery to meet their needs. We believe effective communication does take time. It is a case of whether we choose to invest our time or spend it. Do we choose to invest our time to achieve mutual understanding, or do we take short cuts and then spend time correcting the misunderstandings and the arising problems?

We have a better chance of achieving mutual understanding if we regard the recipient as our client. Our purpose is to reach mutual understanding. As we already know it, we need to clarify not only our thinking, but also the most effective way to deliver the message. Now you may well be saying, 'Sure, that's common sense!' We would be the first to agree with you. In fact, we will feel a sense of disappointment if you have not had that reaction several times during this book. It is all common sense. The frustrating thing is that much of what we are writing about has been known, in some form or other, for hundreds of years. Although it may be common sense, it is not common instinctive practice for the majority of people. Most of these things do not appear to be our default behaviours. We appear to need to work hard at them to develop them as habits. Emotionally, our initial preferences seem to be very different. The following points all help us to stay focused on the recipient as our communications client. Say it in 30 seconds or less, start with the big picture, use the right medium, go at their pace, use their language, summarise and test for understanding.

Say it in 30 seconds or less

If we want clarity, we need brevity. If the recipient's brain has to plough through a mass of complex messages we are less likely to get our point across. This rough rule of thumb challenges us to arrange our thinking before we open our mouth. If we fail to do this we are wasting our client's time. We are also wasting our own resources, as we will usually have to spend more time clarifying our original point. If we fail to make an impact, people are at risk of switching off. Say what you mean, and mean what you say, but think it through before you say it! To help here we need to ask ourselves three questions.

- Why am I communicating this?
- What do I need to achieve?
- Therefore, what are the key points the recipient needs to understand?

Start with the big picture

Effective communication is like a journey. Our objective is to reach the same destination together. If we are giving directions to someone, there are two critical factors at play. Where do we want to get to, and are we both starting from the same point? If other parties are starting from a location different to your own, it is pointless giving them instructions from your starting point. You have to put yourself in their shoes. Similarly, what is likely to happen if you start communicating the details of the journey but the recipients are unclear on the destination you want them to arrive at? Chances are that they will tend to focus on the missing information, for example, why do I need to do that? What for? Why is that the best route? If their minds are grappling with these questions it is unlikely that they will pay much attention to what is being said. This brings us straight back to process thinking. 'The big picture' is nothing more than clarifying the purpose of the communication and the outputs. For example, 'I would like us to discuss the best way to organise the holiday rota. What we need is a system that is fair to everyone but does not put the organisation at risk by having any more than two managers off at any one time.' Similarly, if we are describing something, pictures, drawings or physical examples are usually far more accurate and effective than words. The big picture creates the context for the communication. If recipients are clear about the purpose of the conversation ('why') and the outputs ('what'), their minds are free to concentrate on the process ('how').

Use the right medium

We are blessed with more tools to assist our communication than ever before. However, our choice of tool will help or hinder. If we choose a spanner to saw some wood, we will experience little success and a lot of frustration. If we use the same spanner to hammer a nail in, we may experience success, but it is unlikely to be as effective as using the appropriate hammer. None of this is the spanner's fault. A tool is only as effective as the person using it. Our choice of tool is our responsibility. Email and voicemail are great tools for exchanging data and information. However, we are at risk of using them to kill effective communication. Where mutual understanding is essential, a real-time dialogue is necessary.

Only a fraction of the meaning in our communication is conveyed by the words. The majority is contained in our tone, facial expressions and body language. All of these cues provide the context for the words. Without them the risk of misinterpretation is dramatically increased. If we have clarified the purpose and outputs of our communication, and we treat the recipient as a client, we are more likely to choose the most effective medium. If all we need to do is remind people of an agreed deadline, email may be a brilliant medium. If we want to review someone's performance, email could be a motivational death sentence. Yes, we know it is common sense. But we still observe people sitting five yards away from each other exchanging emails on delicate topics because it is less of a responsibility than truly communicating with each other. When choosing our medium we need to consider the following questions:

- Why am I communicating this?
- What do I need to achieve?
- Therefore, what are the key points the recipient needs to understand?
- How important is it that we achieve mutual understanding?
- What are the consequences if we do not?
- Do we need to meet, video conference, phone, email, fax, write?

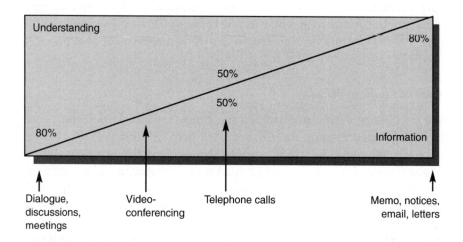

Figure 5.1 Choosing the appropriate medium

Go at their pace

The people we are communicating with are the clients. The pace should be driven by their needs. We already understand the message we want to convey. What is important to the client may differ from what is important to us. Are you going too fast? Too slow? Labouring the point unnecessarily? Causing them to lose the will to live? Watch their non-verbal cues. If you are still unclear, why not ask whether you are going at an appropriate pace?

Use their language

The same applies here. Jargon can be a useful timesaver, but only when both parties understand it. Similarly, talking down to people or using terms that are unfamiliar can cause resentment and frustration. Our aim should be to be clear and user-friendly. Trying to impress or ingratiate ourselves should be low down on the agenda.

Summarise and test for understanding

If we end our conversation without testing whether we have reached mutual understanding, the whole process may be a waste of time. Simply asking the other person to summarise the main points of the conversation can remove many future misunderstandings.

Expectations

> Blessed is he who expects nothing,
> For he shall never be disappointed.
> Alexander Pope, 1727

> It is only because we are ill informed that anything surprises us;
> And we are disappointed because we expect that for which we have not provided.
> Charles Dudley Warner, 1871

Providing clarity on what is expected is a central leadership skill. Empowerment is a much used and possibly abused term these days. It surprises us that managers appear to use the term and yet have been given little guidance on how to create it. It is almost as though it has become a corporate mantra which, if repeated frequently enough, will suddenly spring into reality. We believe that empowerment requires a partnership approach. The leader has to create an appropriate environment for individuals to empower themselves, and the individuals have to choose to be empowered. The two essential threads are clarity on what is expected, in order to create the appropriate environment, and responsibility to encourage individuals to empower themselves. Field Marshall Montgomery felt that he achieved this when he described the relationship he aimed to create with his men: 'I made the soldiers partners with me in the battle. I always told them what I was going to do, and what I wanted them to do. I think the soldiers felt that they mattered, that they belonged.'

One of the key issues with empowerment is knowing where the boundaries are. From the team member's point of view the concerns are usually, 'Can I do whatever I feel is appropriate?' 'What happens if I overstep the mark?' and 'How can I second-guess what the boss wants?' From the leader's perspective, the challenge is articulating what is expected and trusting that the individual will not let you down. Oliver Cromwell understood this leadership requirement. Dr Bate defined one of Cromwell's key attributes when he wrote, 'No man knew more of men.'

A short story illustrates this. Cromwell and Henry Ireton had been stopped by their own guards, and initially the guards refused to believe who they were when they gave them their names. Ireton was annoyed at being given a hard time but Cromwell did not resort to a 'Don't you know who I am?' type of response. Instead he praised the guards for carrying out their duty in a proper way and actually rewarded them by giving them 20 shillings, clearly a motivating and empowering action.

The environment for empowerment is heavily influenced by the clarity of expectations between leaders and their team members. This is broader than agreeing objectives. Objectives are an important focus, but they are not the start point. We believe that there is a hierarchy to clarifying expectations.

Agreeing your relationship

One of the most significant drains on a person's motivation and commitment can be the quality of the relationship with his or her

There are four levels to work at:

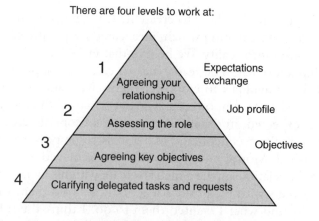

Figure 5.2 Clarity on what is expected as the cornerstone of performance

boss. If people feel valued and respected by their leaders, they are more likely to feel committed and powerful. To create this relationship, both parties need to understand how to get the best from each other. The start point therefore is the clarification of the nature of the relationship. Here leaders should be interested in what kind of working relationship gets the best out of each of their team members. This is also about clarifying what you as the leader do and do not expect of your team members in how they behave. This creates a discussion for what we expect of each other in order to get the best performance we can. It becomes a 'contract' which can be reviewed in order to stimulate continuous improvement in the effectiveness of the relationship.

This is also instrumental in reinforcing the culture that is required for success. It therefore needs to be aligned to the values of the organisation. To make it work, you will need to draw on your graciousness. This is about listening first and not being driven by ego needs to 'lay down the law' because you are the boss. You always have the authority to state your wishes, and to insist on them if appropriate. However, this should be the final point of a full discussion. Our experience is that people are very receptive to exchanging expectations. Both parties learn a lot from it. The relationship tends to move into a new level. As such, having to force home your wishes is a rare event.

Sir Thomas More, when Lord Chancellor, had heard that a number of judges had complained against his injunctions. Rather than dismiss their protests out of hand, More invited the judges to dinner at Westminster. There, painstakingly, he discussed the particular cases of concern in some detail and the judges eventually agreed that had they been in More's place they would have made the same decisions.

More then set out his expectation of the judges, and indicated that if they would act in a reasonable way by using their own discretion more, and change by being more balanced in the way they interpreted the law, then he would not grant any further injunctions. Unfortunately this combined coaching and expectations-setting exercise failed, and in the event the judges were to continue to rely completely on jury verdicts and to interpret the law strictly. Accordingly, during his tenure as Lord Chancellor More received over 900 Chancery petitions per year (compared to just over 500 by his predecessor, Wolsey). Of course, in a normal team leader/team member relationship the judges' response would not have been acceptable, and appropriate action would need to be taken by the team leader.

The modern expectations exchange process is based on the belief that all work relationships, both internal and external, should be viewed in terms of a customer–supplier relationship where all the participants are involved in the search for inefficiency and wastage. It is also useful to look at leader–team member interactions in terms of customer–supplier relationships, with elements of each in both directions. Both parties supply things to each other. The leader supplies information, feedback, coaching, training, resources and support. The team member supplies effort, motivation, commitment, results, information, reports, completed projects and so on.

With all customer–supplier relationships, there is less wastage of resources when there is clarity on what is expected. This requires a process of:

- rigorous agreement and commitment to what each expects from the other
- ongoing review of recent performance to the agreed expectations
- agreed areas for improvement for the future.

There are four basic statements for each party to be clear and in agreement about in order to maximise effectiveness:

- What I expect from you is …
- What I do not expect from you is …
- What you should expect of me is …
- What you should not expect of me is …

Process

The approach is similar whether it is between individuals or groups:

1. Each party should do some work alone to clarify their initial answers to the four questions.
2. Arrange a discussion in a quiet location where you will not be disturbed. The amount of time needed will vary. A minimum of an hour is usually required, if you plan to discuss how both parties are currently performing against the expectations you have just agreed.
3. Team members should always go first. This sends the message that it is a two-way discussion and you value their thoughts. It

114

also avoids you dominating the conversation and encouraging team members to just agree with your views. The important point here is to learn about how they prefer to work with you in order to get the best out of themselves. Once you have listened and understood, you are in a more informed position to decide whether it is feasible or not.

4. The team member explains his or her views on the first statement, 'What I expect of you as my manager is ...'.
5. The manager listens and does not comment, apart from asking for clarification where necessary, until the team member has finished expressing his or her views.
6. The manager then explains his or her views of 'What I think you should expect of me as your manager'.
7. Both parties then compare the similarities in their expectations and discuss and agree a common view.
8. Once both parties are clear that they agree on the expectation, they repeat the process for the remaining questions.

The nature of the content varies according to the people involved, the type and volume of interactions, whether individuals or groups are involved and whether the interaction is internal to the organisation or external. While the focus will move, there should be a combination of behavioural expectations such as openness, integrity, commitment, ownership, reliability and so on, and specific outputs like volume, quality, times and costs.

Due to the group dynamics, and the need for an impartial guide, an experienced facilitator is usually needed when running an expectations exchange between two groups of people.

Responsibility

> Unto whomsoever much is given, of him shall much be required.
> *Luke* 12: 48

We believe that there is a tension in the human condition. Part of our mind wants an easy life, to be free from responsibility, yet responsibility helps us to find meaning in our life. Human beings appear to be 'wired' for achievement. It provides a sense of accomplishment which positively feeds our self-esteem. However, in order to achieve something we first need to accept responsibility for it. We believe that responsibility is a key to motivation. It unlocks the opportunity to accomplish things and to create a positive self-image. If people are clear on what they are responsible for, and have the ability and resources to deliver it, they tend to find it easier to self-motivate.

It seems almost criminal to us that for the best part of the last hundred years, the opposite logic has been used when designing work. The prevailing thinking has focused on breaking down jobs to the point where most people do not have to feel responsible for anything. They just need to do tasks. The responsibility and power is then put into the hands of a few managers. These managers then face an uphill battle to get any discretionary activity from their people by motivating them. This relies on the assumption that motivation is something one person does to another person. This is a false assumption. The only person who can motivate John Barratt is John Barratt. The only person who can motivate Alan Coppin is Alan Coppin; and ultimately the only person who can motivate you is you. In order to do this, we need a sense of responsibility, otherwise there is no reason to bother. Without this sense of responsibility, where is the challenge that moves us out of our comfort zone? There is danger in the comfort zone. If we stay in it for too long we go to sleep. We exist but do not live. We are present but not vital. Regrettably, we feel that this is a common state for too many people at work and in society.

We need to stretch ourselves to feel the sense of accomplishment that fuels our positive self-esteem. However, there is potential danger here also. If we are over-stretched for too long we experience panic.

The only person who can motivate me is me.
There is a need to accept responsibility for my own energy level.
However, the environment I am in will either help me to charge myself up, or it might be a constant drain.

A positive environment helps me to motivate myself

Unsupportive, restrictive and unfulfilling environments drain: I have to work unnecessarily hard to stay positive

Our role as leaders is to create a positive environment

Figure 5.3 Motivation is a form of energy

If panic and stress become our normal state we are at risk of being inefficient and ineffective. We have passed our 'elastic limit' for that moment in time and cease to feel positive and alive. Indeed, we can feel ill.

We view motivation as a form of energy. It is present in all of us, possibly in varying quantities. Only individuals can tap into this energy, but the environment they live and work in can either help or hinder them to stay 'positively charged'.

An environment where people find it easier to stay positively charged is usually characterised by individuals having a high level of responsibility and authority (within guidelines and with training) for the decisions and outputs of their work. Individuals feel able to use their talents and creativity in their jobs. They experience themselves as continuously learning, growing and improving. This can be a challenge for managers and team members, as it calls for different thinking and behaviour from both parties. From team leaders' perspectives, they need to see their role more as a coach than a law enforcer, coordinating rather than controlling. This relies on a different skill set: the ability to listen, question, coach, encourage and facilitate. From team members' points of view, they need to acknowledge their right and their responsibility for improving things. This can be a significant leap if an individual has been schooled in the belief that improvement is exclusively the work of managers. Here people usually need clarity on what they are responsible for, and some guidance in how to apply some problem solving tools.

As leaders, we benefit greatly if we are clear and explicit about who has the responsibility for things. Without this clarity, ownership of the issue becomes clouded. A team member may think that he or she has no responsibility for an issue. The team leader may think that the team member has full responsibility for it. The usual consequence of this situation involves nothing being done, a sharp exchange of views and the team leader muttering, 'Do I have to do everything around here?' However, for much of the time team leaders are likely to be creating the situation by not holding people responsible.

In order to encourage people to take the initiative, the initiative needs to be given to them in the first place. In other words, the responsibility for resolving the problem should stay with the team member, and he or she should be absolutely clear about this. This seems obvious. However, consider the familiar case where a team (or family) member comes to you to discuss a problem. You want to be helpful, but you have not got the time or the information to make a decision right now. So you say something like, 'Leave it with me.' At this moment, who owns the responsibility for fixing the problem? The other person will probably leave the room believing that he or she has fulfilled his/her responsibility. In his/her perception you will now fix it. Meanwhile it gets added to your 'do this when you can fit it in' pile and your stress level moves one imperceptible notch higher. As you struggle to find the time to address the issue, the other person becomes frustrated with the lack of progress and disenchanted with you as a consequence.

People are paid to be responsible. They are paid to solve the problems that are an inherent part of their job. In wanting to be helpful, we risk removing this responsibility from them. If they have little responsibility, they have little challenge. If they have little challenge, they become comfortable. If they are comfortable for too long, they go to sleep. If they are asleep, you end up doing their job for them. If you do their job for them, they feel even less responsible.

The role of a leader is to offer help, *without taking away responsibility*. In other words, team (or family) members understand that it is their responsibility to resolve the problem, but you will assist them by listening to understand, and through coaching and encouragement if needed.

The influence of the monarch on politics in the eighteenth and early nineteenth century was, of course, rather different from today. One of the powers which George III had was the appointment of ministers, but once appointed, he allowed them to get on with the business of government. A leading politician of the time, Lord Hillsborough, acknowledged this quality in the King when he said, 'The King will always leave his own sentiments and conform to his Ministers, though he will argue with them very sensibly. But if they adhere to their own opinion, he will say "Well. Do you choose it to be so? Then let it be."' The King himself later described his role as keeping a 'superintending eye' upon his government.

Allowing and delegating

We will return to coaching in Chapter 6, 'Mutuality'. In this section, we want to dwell on two vital components for encouraging responsibility: allowing and delegating. The two are heavily connected. If we delegate work to a colleague, but do not allow him or her the chance of success, we are setting him or her up for failure. If this is a regular occurrence, it usually discourages the individual from seeking responsibility in the future. Allowing is concerned with creating the climate for success. This means working hard to provide the resources and authority to give the person the tools to complete the delegated work. If we ask someone to complete a task, but do not provide him or her with the decision making authority or the resources to do it, we are encouraging failure.

Our intention may be to energise the person by providing a new challenge, but if we go not give him or her the decision making authority or the resources to do it, we are likely to have the opposite effect. This means 'clearing the way' by notifying the relevant people that the individual concerned is authorised to act, and by providing access to the budget, people and resources required. The final critical thing to remember is that while you must delegate the responsibility and the authority, the ultimate accountability remains with you. Gino Watkins, a polar explorer in the 1930s ranking alongside Sir Ernest Shackleton and Captain Robert Scott, understood where the buck stopped. His management style was captured by J. M. Scott in his biography of Watkins, when he wrote:

> If he told inexperienced men to do what they thought best, and if they made some fatal blunder, the responsibility would be his just as surely as if he had expressly ordered that disastrous action. The world would see it thus and so would he. It was a risky policy, but for his purpose the risk was unavoidable.

You chose to delegate the work; you should not blame the individual if it fails to work out the way you want. Hold them responsible for sure, but never blame them publicly to save your own face. This is a surefire way to earn a reputation as an untrustworthy leader. General Robert E. Lee, one of the great military leaders in the American Civil War, showed how he appreciated this notion when he responded to a distraught and angry officer, angry at the losses of his men: 'General, all this has been my fault. It is I who have lost this fight and you must help me out of it the best way you can.'

Delegation is a term frequently used by busy managers in the process of their working day. We find that there is confusion over delegation and abdication. Driven by day to day pressures, busy managers can easily fall into the twin pits of ineffective delegation: 'dumping' and 'avoiding'. Dumping is usually driven by a need to get things off your 'to do' list as fast as possible. It is centred around your needs and often involves the jobs that you find tedious. Little explanation or support is offered, and it runs the risk of being a draining experience for the recipient. Avoiding is based on the feeling that it is faster to get things done yourself, and you may doubt the ability of anyone else to complete the task. While this can be very true in the short term, if it becomes the long-term way of working it condemns you to a high work load and denies your team members the opportunity for stretch and growth. An important part of delegation is developing team members so that they have the capability to receive more challenging work from you.

To practise the rewarding skill of effective delegation, you will need to make the time and commitment to do it. There are also a number of perceived barriers to delegating. These usually include the following perceptions.

- Where do I find the time?
- I do not trust the team members to do a good job.
- I fear that my team members may appear better than me, or may steal the glory.
- I still enjoy the technical features of my previous job, and want to carry on doing it.
- I take refuge in being busy doing jobs which are easy.
- I am flattered when team members delegate jobs back to me because they do not know how to do them. It makes me feel useful and important.

The majority of these barriers are emotional. They are normal reactions to change. However, to overcome them, we need an incentive. So why bother? Well, we believe that it offers a number of significant benefits.

Avoid drowning in other people's work

In a fast-moving world, managers are continually acquiring new responsibilities. It is easy to work at the wrong level, especially if you have been telling team members to 'leave things with you' for quite a while. If you do not let go of some of them you will drown.

There are three steps here. First, determine which aspects of your work can be stopped completely, as they no longer add any value. Second, encourage all your team members to do this and agree it with you. Third, delegate the work that is better suited to the responsibilities of your team members.

You can fully utilise the specialist skills of the team members

There may be people in your team who are better at things than you are. This leads to efficiencies and improved outputs.

You have more time for planning and innovation

If you are spending all your time working 'in' the business, who is working 'on' it? Where will problem prevention and process improvement come from?

You are not trapped in your job

If you have developed your people through delegation and coaching, you will be more likely to have a capable person to succeed you. If this is in place, your promotion chances may be enhanced.

Increased motivation and commitment from team members

Most people are achievement oriented. Helping people to achieve is rewarding in its own right. However, recruitment and retention of capable people becomes easier as well.

Our observation is that delegation is frequently misunderstood and ineffectively applied. Our definition of effective delegation is 'giving a team member the responsibility, authority and support to handle certain matters on his/her own initiative, with the confidence that he/she can do the job successfully'. To apply this in practice we suggest the following guidelines.

Guidelines for effective delegation.

- *Clarify their specific responsibility.* Provide a team member with a meaningful and recognisable element of the company's activity. Ideally, the connection between this activity and the team or company purpose and vision should be clear and explicit. Specify the measurable output that is required.
- *Clarify the individual's authority with him or her and with all other colleagues who are key to success.* Give the team member permission to control resources and make changes and decisions

within specified limits, so that he or she can achieve the results required.

- *Retain the reins.* Agree clear standards of performance for the different stages of work. Establish a process of monitoring and reviewing progress with the individual.
- *Retain accountability.* Hold the team member responsible for the consequences of his/her actions, but accept and demonstrate that ultimate accountability still rests with the delegator.
- *Be clear what to delegate.* In general terms you should delegate aspects of your job:
  - where the team member can do it better, quicker or more cheaply
  - where it means you can be freed to spend time on more important tasks
  - where it can develop the team member.
- *Delegate whole tasks, consistently.* Both good and bad tasks should be delegated and spread out among the team.
- *Do it* with *people not* to *them.*

These principles can be applied by using the simple framework outlined in the 'Toolbox' section.

 ## Clarity: key points

Communication

- Much effort is wasted due to a lack of clarity.
- We need to be able to align people's roles and skills on the right things. Without this, committed people will do the wrong things right.
- Effective communication is the lifeblood of any relationship.
- High performance needs everyone to accept their responsibility for effective communication.
- The essence of effective communication is mutual understanding.
- The major shift in thinking needed is 'to think like a supplier'. The recipient is our 'communications client'.
- Stay focused on the recipient as our communications client by
  - saying it in 30 seconds or less

- starting with the big picture
- using the right medium
- going at their pace
- using their language
- summarising and testing for understanding.

- Achieving mutual understanding needs a communications partnership. The speaker needs to be clear and concise in his or her expression. The recipient needs to listen to understand.
- Listening to people is a mark of respect. It signals to them that we value them enough to choose to give them our attention. The opposite is also true.
- Effective listening requires us to listen with our minds. We have to be fully focused in our head as well as our ears. Listen generously.
- Effective listening builds trust and cooperation.
- Our focus should be on finding the most appropriate solution, rather than wasting time trying to win the argument.

Expectations

- The environment for empowerment is heavily influenced by the clarity of expectations between leaders and their team members.
- If people feel valued and respected by their leader, they are more likely to feel committed and powerful. To create this relationship, both parties need to understand how to get the best from each other.
- All work relationships, both internal and external, should be viewed in terms of a customer–supplier relationship where all the participants are involved in removing inefficiency and wastage.
- There is less wastage of resources when there is clarity on what is expected.

Responsibility

- Responsibility is a key to motivation. It unlocks the opportunity to accomplish things and to create a positive self-image.

- If people are clear on what they are responsible for and have the ability and resources to deliver it, they tend to find it easier to self-motivate.
- We view motivation as a form of energy. It is present in all of us, possibly in varying quantities. Only individuals can tap into this energy, but the environment they live and work in can either help or hinder them to stay 'positively charged'.
- An environment where people find it easier to stay 'positively charged' is usually characterised by individuals having a high level of responsibility and authority (within guidelines and with training) for the decisions and outputs of their work.
- This can be a challenge for managers and team members, as it calls for different thinking and behaviour from both parties.
- People are paid to be responsible. They are paid to solve the problems that are an inherent part of their job.
- In wanting to be helpful we risk removing this responsibility from people.
- The role of a leader is to offer help, without taking away responsibility.

Allowing and delegating

- If we delegate work to a colleague, but do not allow him or her the chance of success, we are setting him/her up for failure.
- If we ask someone to complete a task, but do not provide him or her with the decision making authority or the resources to do it, we are encouraging failure.
- While you must delegate the responsibility and the authority, the ultimate accountability remains with you.
- An important part of delegation is developing team members so that they have the capability to receive more challenging work from you.
- To practise the rewarding skill of effective delegation, you will need to make the time and commitment to do it.

Clarity toolbox

Developing your empathic listening skills

The following skills are easy to understand but require lifelong practice!

Skill	Example
Summarising and testing understanding This demonstrates that you really are listening and also reduces the chances of the communication process being derailed due to assumptions. Use your own words or you sound like a parrot!	'As I understand it, what you are saying is …' 'Do you mean that …?' 'So your point is that …'
Inviting further contributions This is used to help clarify your understanding, and to avoid assuming that the way you perceive things is the same as the way the other person perceives things. Open-ended requests to say more are generally preferable to pointed questions. Probing questions may lead to the speaker feeling pushed.	'Tell me a bit more about that.' 'How did you feel when …?' 'How did it come about that …?' 'What happened then?'
Reflecting the underlying feelings This aims to encourage the speaker to surface the feelings, attitudes, beliefs or values which underpin their perceptions. The objective is to empathise, to emotionally put yourself in the place of the speaker, to experience how it must feel to be in their situation.	'You sound annoyed/disappointed/let down.' 'If that happened to me, I'd be upset.' 'Times when I've been in that sort of situation, I've really felt I could use some help.' 'If I achieved that, I'd feel proud of myself.' 'That must have been satisfying.'

Reflecting the implications

This involves building on or extending the ideas of the speaker. It is important when reflecting the implications to leave the speaker in control of the discussion. You are prompting in order to encourage further clarity or exploration of the other person's thinking.

'I guess if you did that, you'd then be in a position to …'
'So that might lead to a situation in which …'
'Would that mean that …?'
'Are you suggesting that we might …?'
'Would that help with the problem of …?'

Non-verbal listening responses

Active listening is often communicated as much by posture and non-verbal movements as by words. Even if you are listening attentively, the other person will assume that you are not if your body language sends that message.

Looking the speaker in the eyes. It is hard to believe someone is listening if he or she is looking off into space.
Nodding and making receptive noises (e.g. 'Aha').
Leaning towards the speaker, and looking alert.

A simple and effective process for improved delegation

- **Explain the background and why it is important.**
- **Agree the desired result:**
    - Focus on what not how.
    - Be specific and make it measurable in terms of quantity, quality, time, cost and behaviour.
    - Ask the person to summarise it to test his/her understanding.
- **Highlight any dangers or pitfalls to be avoided.**
    - Point out what they should avoid, not what they must do.
- **Highlight the resources that are available to them if they need them:** financial, technical and people.
- **Discuss the consequences.**
    - Explain what will happen as a result of this job being completed:

	Successful	*Unsuccessful*
– for the organisation	Benefit	Risk
– for the individual	Benefit (reward)	Risk

- **Agree key 'milestone' meetings if necessary.**
  - Guide the pace by agreeing 'deadlines' for key steps in the journey.
  - This also helps reassure you that the person will not 'go off like a loose cannon'.
- **Summarise.** Ask the other person to summarise the discussion.

Timeless Management historical illustrations

Timeless Manager 7: Duke Of Wellington – clarity

Arthur Wellesley, 1st Duke of Wellington (1769–1852). British general, statesman and Prime Minister (1828–30), born in Dublin, Ireland.

Connections with Historic Royal Palaces

During his term as Constable of the Tower of London, from 1826 until 1840, Wellington was responsible for some dramatic changes to the fortress. He modernised the terms of employment of the Yeoman Warders, finally abolishing the process by which posts were passed down from father to son. After it emerged that 80 members of the Tower garrison were in hospital because of the poor quality of the water supply and a report was made describing the moat as 'impregnated with putrid animal and excrementitious matter', Wellington took the momentous decision to drain the great medieval moat of the Tower in 1843. Also to improve conditions for soldiers in the fortress, Wellington oversaw the construction of an enormous new building which was to provided barrack accommodation for 1,000 men. In 1845 he laid the foundation stone of the building, which was to be named, after his most famous victory, the Waterloo Barracks.

On his death, Wellington was given a lavish and elaborate state funeral. Queen Victoria gave specific instructions about what was to happen to his funeral car: 'It is her Majesty's wish that the funeral car with its appurtenances should be deposited in the Tower and that it should there be exhibited to the Public.' Objects associated with him, including his uniform, were displayed in the Tower throughout the rest of the nineteenth and twentieth centuries.

Historical illustration

Born in 1769 the same year as Napoleon Bonaparte, even at birth Wellington was ahead of his arch rival – by just over three months.

These two major figures were to have more than just a birth year in common: they were of course both masters in generalship (albeit with different leadership styles) and they even shared two mistresses!

As a boy Arthur Wesley's future looked far from promising, and his eventual retitling, first as Wellesley and then as Wellington, the Iron Duke, could never have been predicted. He was a poor scholar and cut a lonely figure at Eton, apparently preferring his own company to the gregarious school games of the time. When family finances became stretched, Arthur was removed from Eton in favour of his younger and brighter brother, Henry.

Following a period in Brussels with his mother, the young Wesley was enrolled in the Angers Military Academy in France. His mother had a rather unhealthy disdain for her sixth child and is famously quoted as saying that her 'ugly boy Arthur was food for powder and nothing more'. Thus started the career of one of the most successful generals and eminent figures in British history, who was described following his death in 1852 by Queen Victoria as 'the greatest man this country ever produced'.

A key factor in his success as a soldier, and later in his life as politician and eventually as Prime Minister, was his clarity, and his succinct and well-considered opinions were highly valued. This quality was a key differentiator between the Iron Duke and his adversary Napoleon. One of his admirers was William Pitt, Prime Minister who said of him:

> He never makes a difficulty or hides his ignorance in vague generalities. If I put a question to him he answers it distinctly; if I wanted an explanation he gave it clearly; if I desired an opinion I got from him one supported by reasons which were always sound. He states every difficulty before he undertakes any service, but never after he has undertaken it.

Wellington himself recognised the need for clarity when he said, 'There is nothing in life like a clear definition.' He applied this clarity to communication in his despatches, and these contrasted with the confused and difficult to read despatches sent by Napoleon. So well written were these despatches that some years later one of the Duke's junior officers in the Peninsular war put together a publication featuring excerpts from his despatches together with his general orders. On reviewing the work Wellington himself commented, 'I was quite surprised ... to see how well they were written.... I had at the time all the care and foresight and attention to detail that could forward the business which I had in charge.'

It was also his clarity of thinking that set Wellington apart from other mere mortals. This could be seen on the battlefield, in quickly evaluating situations and modifying his plans accordingly. This clear thinking is also portrayed as basic common sense and the power of seeing things as they are, interpreting them, drawing conclusions and taking action. This is demonstrated by his succinct analysis of the key difference between the Napoleonic and Wellington war machines: 'The French planned their campaigns just as you might make a splendid piece of harness; it looks very well until it get broken and then you are done for. Now I make my campaigns of ropes. If anything went wrong, I tied a knot and went on.'

Wellington believed very much in leading by example, being in the thick of battle at some considerable personal danger. He would take personal responsibility for his actions and was known to take over command at critical moments. But he was also able to delegate and allow his officers to experience command. He almost certainly did this at Nive in Spain when he allowed Generals Hope and Hill to control the campaign. And he showed his confidence in General Freire and the Spaniards under his command at San Marcial. He also saw the requirement for accountability and delegation in the structure of the army, and while engaged in action in Portugal he introduced the then revolutionary concept of autonomous divisions.

However, he was also quick to take charge and to be accountable. In December 1803, following his famous victory at Assaye in India, Wellesley was in charge of a mixed army including Sepoys who had served so well at Assaye. At one stage his army, which was facing a larger force of Mahrathas, was in some disarray. Wellesley calmly took charge of the situation and the resulting conflict was impressively won. After the battle, his succinct evaluation was: 'If I had not been there ... we should have lost the day.'

Wellington recognised the power of communication not just in the concise despatches he wrote but also in listening. This was one key competitive advantage he enjoyed. He recognised 'the want of information by the enemy's General officers' and is quoted as saying, 'Everywhere I received intelligence from the peasants and priests. The French learnt nothing.'

During the Peninsular campaign in Portugal, Wellington saw the sense of close affiliation with the 'irregular' Portuguese partisans.

These were part of the intelligence gathering operation and would intercept French despatches. Eventually these partisans were 'regularised' under the command of British scouts, probably the forerunner of the Intelligence Corps or even Intelligence services.

One made-up newspaper story of the time demonstrates the clarity of the Iron Duke's thinking, or at least the popular perception of it. At the time of the Great Exhibition in 1851 Wellington was a national hero, and one of a number of honours bestowed on him was Ranger of the Royal Parks, which included responsibility for Hyde Park, site of the Great Exhibition. He was not initially a great supporter of this daring project (although later like most of the population he became a convert).

The centrepiece of the Great Exhibition was the Crystal or Glass Palace. Within this building was a large tree, because one condition of holding the event in Hyde Park was that no trees should be cut down. A major problem resulting from this was the large number of sparrows who had been enclosed in the structure along with the tree. Their droppings landed on the thousands of objects that were being displayed in the building. The Queen, no less, allegedly asked for solutions to this rather annoying problem. The first response was 'shoot them'. It was then realised that this was impractical, since the glass panes forming the building would also be shattered. The next was to coat the trees with birdlime, but by this time the sparrows were using the iron girders instead of the tree branches. When Wellington was asked for his opinion he was insulted and initially considered responding that 'he is not a bird catcher'. However, he is supposed to have gone to the palace to have delivered his solution direct to the Queen: 'Try sparrow hawks, Ma'am.'

In his lifetime the Duke of Wellington amassed nearly 70 titles and honours including of course, Prime Minister, Foreign Secretary and Commander in Chief of the British Army. He reached this position of eminence by being himself at all times. Wellington was truly his own man. In this respect clarity can describe his approach to life, and he is often described as being transparent. In modern day parlance, 'what you see is what you get'. One of his friends, G. R. Gleig, described this aspect of Wellington's character as being 'more completely free from disguise' than any other great person.

At his funeral 1.5 million people watched the funeral procession and there was an outpouring of public grief. What a transformation of the boy who had little scholastic ability and who, according to his own mother, was only fit for cannon fodder.

Timeless Manager 8: William I – responsibility

William I (of England) (1028–1087), known as William the Conqueror. Duke of Normandy (1035–87) and the first Norman King of England (1066–87).

Connections with Historic Royal Palaces

Duke William of Normandy started building castles in England immediately after the Battle of Hastings in 1066, to enable him to control and colonise the land he had conquered. Securing London, the most powerful city in England, was of the first importance to the Conqueror, and in the 1070s he started work on an enormous building in the south-eastern corner of the Roman city walls constructed specifically to overawe the 'vast and fierce' population of London. This building, the White Tower of the Tower of London, was completed after William's death, in about 1100, and was quite unlike anything that had ever been built in England before. It was both a huge defensive keep and a royal residential building, provided with great fireplaces, privies and an exquisite Norman chapel. It is the oldest building within the Tower of London and is perhaps the most perfect example of the Norman style of architecture brought over by William remaining in England.

Historical illustration

History, in one particular respect, has been kind to William I. To the modern age he is universally known by his positive nickname 'the Conqueror', whereas his contemporaries referred to him as 'William the Bastard'. Undoubtedly his illegitimacy fired his ambition and spurred him to great and at times ruthless achievements. But it is his characteristic of responsibility, rather than his parentage, that is our focus.

When he invaded England in 1066 William was about 38 years old (his exact date of birth is not known) and yet he had ruled Normandy for more than half his life and therefore had significant experience as a military commander and leader of a realm. This was an excellent proving ground for his post-1066 activities.

Both in France and after the conquest of England William displayed exemplary skills as a commander in battle, and this is where his aptitude for leading by example can best be demonstrated. He rode to where the arrows were flying. There are a number of accounts of

William's leadership and bravery in the thick of battle, but the one chosen as the most appropriate happened during the Battle of Hastings.

The immediate military background to this battle is that the army of Harold I had marched from York where it had recently won another battle, ostensibly against Norwegian invaders. Amazingly the march covered about 250 miles in only 13 days, which included a stop-over in London to recruit more men. So on arrival in Hastings the army must have been rather weary. By contrast William's army had a fortnight to prepare for battle after its meticulously planned and fortuitous (the wind changed) crossing of the English Channel. Nevertheless, in terms of resources the two sides were evenly matched, with about 7,000 men in each army.

The Battle of Hastings lasted all day, having started at about 9.00 am, and during that time William's involvement can be evidenced by the three horses he was riding that were killed. A defining moment in the battle came when a rumour was spread around the field of battle that William had been killed. William's leadership and personal example were critical to his force, and had this rumour not been stamped on there could have been a different outcome to the battle and, indeed, the history of England. William's immediate response to hearing the rumour was to take off his helmet. This had the desired effect of quashing the rumour and preventing the panic among his army that eventually infected the English army when Harold was subsequently killed (with a sword, and not as is popularly thought by an arrow through the eye).

Once the Battle of Hastings was over, the task Duke William had first in conquering and then in ruling a foreign country was manifestly difficult. In a way the Battle of Hastings and military conquest were the easy part. The difficult part was how to govern England, and William decided on a system that was basically aristocratic colonisation.

In order to proceed with the invasion William had to convince an uncertain Norman aristocracy which itself had been involved in a long-running series of territorial disputes. The result of these often bloody disputes was the supremacy of the Duke of Normandy, William. The method of William's organisation of Normandy was to act as a blue-print for his subsequent management of England. Effectively Normandy was divided into a number of specific areas each governed by a count. The counts were given clear responsibility for the manage-ment of their own areas, including security, tax collection and the administration of justice. They were required to come together to protect their country in the event of attack from outside. It was an early federal system, made all the more secure for William by his appointment to key posts of his family and friends.

Once England had been conquered, William was able to establish a similar system, and rewarded his loyal Norman aristocracy by parcelling up large areas for them to oversee and personally benefit from. These included William Fitz Osbern who become Earl of Hereford, and another two Normans were made Earls of Shrewsbury and Chester.

William I attempted to simplify and clarify the roles of the courts, which in the eleventh century were central to the government of the country. In order to do this William empowered the sheriffs to oversee and supervise the organisation of justice in the existing confusing county and hundred courts. However, in the event William needed to control the sheriffs themselves (since they used their positions to increase their own wealth) and this he did by dispatching his own trusted aides to conduct the most important trials.

William I certainly pioneered the ultimate mechanism for personal/legal responsibility: the jury system, although this was a far cry from our current system. In William's time 'juries of inquest' were established, which were merely required to swear the truth about the fact. For example juries of local people were sworn in to provide information for the compilation of the *Domesday Book*.

In eleventh century terms William the Conqueror and his delegated team were able, after a time, to create conditions of peace and order throughout the country.

There were a number of reasons that William, the Duke of a much smaller 'country', was able to conquer England, and undoubtedly his success in his choice of those reporting to him and the clarity of his instructions to them were key. But there were other reasons, too. William oversaw the completion of over 80 castles during the course of his reign, and they were to enable his chosen supporters to dominate the land around. Perhaps most important, at times William I invoked terror on his subjects. In doing this he went beyond normal warfare and devastated the lives of thousands of ordinary people. Allegedly, he was to regret these actions when on his deathbed he said, 'I persecuted the native inhabitants of England beyond all reason.... I cruelly oppressed them.... I am stained with the rivers of blood that I have shed.' Perhaps a bastard in more ways than one.

6 Mutuality

There is no they, only us.
Anon.

High performance relies on commitment. Commitment is a voluntary quality. People have to choose to be committed: you cannot force it, that would be coercion. There usually needs to be a reason to choose to commit. Perhaps it is the power of the vision, the graciousness of the leader, or a desire to test and prove oneself. Whatever the initial reason, it tends to be sustained only if there is a continued sense of worth and ownership: a sense that the individual is part of something important and worthy, a mutual endeavour with mutual benefits. This notion was brilliantly and simply captured by Sir Isaac Newton, when he wrote in a letter to Robert Hooke in February 1676, 'If I have seen further it is by standing on the shoulders of giants.' Some historians believe this was an ironic comment of Newton's, but we believe it captures the essence of mutuality.

Oliver Cromwell on the other hand voiced the frustration of numerous managers when during a speech in the House of Commons, he declared, 'I am as for consent as any man, but where shall it be found?' Hopefully in the next few pages some answers will be given to this rhetorical question, starting with identifying the key components of mutuality, which are:

- trust and synergy
- win–win
- coaching
- review
- recognition
- fun.

Trust and synergy

> Trust men and they will be true to you; treat them greatly and they will show themselves great.
>
> Emersen, 1841

Trust is a vital component for high performance. It feeds commitment and ownership and reduces the amount of time and energy wasted in suspicion and politics. This time and effort can therefore be better deployed on added value activities that help to deliver the purpose and vision. When trust and competence and alignment come together we can achieve synergy, the power of achieving more than the individuals could achieve by themselves. This is the key that unlocks high performance. The outputs of a collection of suspicious but skilled individuals is likely to be less than that of a team of skilled aligned people who trust each other. The nature of their communication and cooperation adds another level to their ability to efficiently and effectively deliver the required results. Alignment comes from a shared purpose and vision. Competence is developed through appropriate selection, training and coaching.

High performance = alignment + competence + trust

We will discuss coaching as a separate section. Before we do that, we believe it is important to consider the foundation stone of trust.

Consider two different people. The first you trust, the second you do not. How do you *feel* when you are dealing with the person you trust? How do you behave when you are talking to him or her? Now think about the person you do not trust. How do you feel when you are dealing with this person? How do you behave when you are talking to him or her? How much do you really want to help the person that you mistrust? Now consider things from the other side of the fence. How will people feel if they do not trust you? How will they behave towards you? How much will they really want to help you?

Trust is the powerhouse for relationships and high performance. A group of people can be aligned but not 'attuned'. They can be an aligned group of individuals but still fall short of being an effective team. We believe an aligned group becomes 'attuned' when the members of the group genuinely care about one another and understand, support and develop each other in the achievement of their individual and team goals. To develop into an attuned team, the members of the group have to be able to trust each other.

Trust is cultivated when people do what they say they will do and act with integrity. To act with integrity we often need to draw on moral courage in order to be honest with others and ourselves. We also need to use our empathic listening skills to understand and value others, as well as draw on our graciousness when receiving feedback. The combination of these factors helps to engender trust and a strong sense of mutuality.

To develop and sustain trust, our words and actions need to be aligned. We also need to be worthy of the trust. If we fail to deliver on a promise, or betray a confidence, why should anyone trust us?

To summarise, trust:

- means people know they can rely on each other
- is vital to constructive relationships and goodwill
- is based on managers being honest, consistent, realistic, following through and acting fairly and decently
- is a personal decision, built when managers behave with integrity and principle
- once destroyed, can only be rebuilt with painful slowness
- when lacking can destroy effective communication, as no one believes what is said.

Creation of trust, along with supportive teamwork, is key to restoring morale and enthusiasm to a team, department or organisation.

Win–win

As with everything in this book, mutuality starts from a shift in thinking. In this case, the shift relates to 'win–win' thinking. In our experience, this is contrary to the 'win–lose' thinking which appears dominant in many cultures. At the heart of 'win–lose' thinking is the assumption that the only way for me to win is to beat someone. In other words, for me to get what I want, I have to deprive someone else. 'Win–win' thinking comes from a different angle. It is based on the belief that there is 'enough to go around', that I can get what I want without depriving others of what they want. This is well understood in Chinese culture in a mind-set comprising values and behaviours called 'Lao Pengyou'. It describes a mutually beneficial partnership for life as opposed to a short-term business relationship. Win–win is the philosophy of mutual gain. Win–lose is one of rivalry. Win–win values relationships and the long term, win–lose is driven by ego and short-term results. Over time, win–lose becomes lose–lose. Both parties become focused on damaging the other. The original purpose and outputs are forgotten, and effort is put into looking better than the others, rather than on finding an appropriate solution.

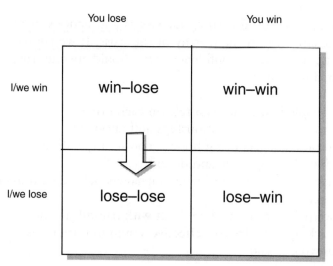

Over time win–lose becomes lose–lose as trust breaks down

Figure 6.1 Mutuality is based on a philosophy of abundance: we can both gain by working with each other

Win–lose situations pervade our culture. In the law courts we use the adversary system. In politics, parties strive to win elections, even at the apparent expense of long-term economic progress. Debates are common at schools, universities and in the media, at the expense of developing real listening skills. The put-down is generally regarded as wit, valuing the short-term 'victory' over the long-term relationship. Indeed, every aspect of work and social life is full of win–lose terms. In such an environment it is easy to apply competitive behaviours where they are inappropriate. For instance, our competitive win–lose thinking undermines our effective listening. We are more interested in winning the point than genuinely understanding the other person's point of view and feelings. Huge amounts of energy are wasted in organisations due to unhealthy competition between individuals and departments. This type of energy is difficult to measure. If we did choose to measure it, it would be interesting to see how much effort and time is used in inappropriate competition, especially if this could be expressed as a percentage of the time and effort used actually to deliver the outputs of the organisation.

Win–lose thinking and behaviour can lead to:

- time and energy being diverted from the main issues
- decisions being delayed
- ineffective listening
- restricting the exploration of alternatives
- reduced sensitivity
- members 'switching off'
- anger and frustration
- the 'losers' feeling resentful
- conscious and unconscious sabotage
- personal acrimony
- defensiveness
- the driving out of common sense.

Competitive spirit is obviously important. However, before we apply our competitive behaviours we believe we should ask some simple questions of ourselves.

- What am I trying to achieve?
- Is competition appropriate?
- Will it achieve the most effective result?
- Who are we competing against and why?
- If we win and they lose, what are the consequences for the long term?

Other actions we can take to reduce our susceptibility to inappropriate win–lose behaviour are:

- Use effective listening to really understand what the other person(s) think(s).
- Use expectations exchanges to establish mutual needs, clear expectations and joint benefits.

- Avoid dogmatic statements. 'One option would be to ...' leaves more room for developing an idea than 'This is the only solution ...'.
- Involve those who will be affected by the decision or change, and involve them early enough that they still feel able to influence events.
- Watch people's body language to check if their words and their non-verbal behaviour are aligned. What you think is a win–win might still be perceived as a win–lose by the other party.

Coaching

> Mankind have been created for the sake of one another.
> Either instruct them, therefore, or endure them.
>
> Marcus Aurelius (AD 121–180)

> Tell me and I'll forget; show me and I may remember; involve me and I'll understand.
>
> Chinese proverb

> If you are too busy to help those around you succeed you're too busy.
>
> Anon.

If managers effectively coached their team members, most management trainers would be looking for other jobs. A sobering thought, especially for John. However, experience suggests that it is not likely to worry him for some years to come. There is no doubt, however, that coaching by an effective manager is the most powerful form of development, just as there is no doubt that the manager is the most powerful influence on how any individual does his or her job. One of the most valuable things that can happen early in someone's career is to work for a boss who is an effective coach. So what do we mean by 'an effective coach?' We are talking about a boss who spends time and planned effort on helping team members to develop, using real situations and treating the process as virtually a continuous one.

Coaching is not a question of descending from time to time to see what a team member is doing and telling them not to. Still less is it the fatherly expression of hard-gained experience, instructing the team member what to do, and throwing in a short pep talk for good measure. It is about raising awareness of how the team or individual is performing, stimulating people to think about this and using situations as they arise and effective questions to provide development opportunities.

On occasions the Duke of Wellington would coach by acting himself. One of Wellington's officers had returned empty-handed from a trip to procure forage from the estate of a Spanish noble. Wellington asked him why he had been unsuccessful. The officer replied that he was told that he would have to bow to the noble Spaniard and that was something, of course, that he would not do. Wellington responded by saying that he supposed he must get the forage himself. Soon carts full of forage were being received in the camp. On being asked how he achieved this, Wellington said, 'Oh, I just bobbed down.' The Duke did not berate or order his officer, he simply used the situation to demonstrate by example how results could be achieved: a powerful method of instruction.

Coaching is based on promoting discovery. The objective is to expand people's knowledge and experience by provoking thought and sharing your experiences. The range of opportunities is huge, ranging from conversations and review events through to coaching individuals through specific projects. It can also include shadowing a boss in a structured way. For example, you could invite a team member to accompany you to a meeting. Before the meeting you could discuss how to prepare, what you want to achieve, the options for achieving it, and potential obstacles and how to overcome them. After the meeting you could ask the team member to review his or her observations and learning. What worked and why? What could have been done differently and how?

The main opportunities for coaching are major events. These can be major events for the team member, or something happening in the department as a whole. Other opportunities come from delegating an aspect of your role. Every situation offers coaching possibilities, but some have more possibilities than others. There is a strong link here with reviewing. Reviewing why things have happened and searching for improvements are great coaching opportunities: the coach and team member can learn together. Once the causes are understood, skilful questioning can promote discovery of options for improvement in the future. This is usually a challenging and rewarding experience for both parties, leading to mutual learning.

Six principles for effective coaching

1. *The purpose of coaching is to* develop *knowledge, skills and attitudes in the other person.* It is not a stage for your ego.

2. *Effective coaching is based on questions.* The aim is to encourage other people to think things through for themselves. Once they have done this they will be more able to transfer this learning to other situations without reference to you.

3. *Where needed, share your experience, both positive and negative.* While coaching is primarily a question-based process, there is no point in continuing to ask questions if the situation is beyond the other person's experience. When he or she runs out of ideas, introduce a thought or a number of possible options and then ask the person to think through his or her preference. If you see the person heading for a pitfall, ask him/her to consider the consequences of these actions, to encourage him/her to think it through. Occasionally it will be useful to share some of your own direct experiences. For instance, if the person you are coaching has not seen the need to rehearse before an important presentation, you could share what happened to you in the past when you failed to rehearse. This appropriate self-disclosure improves the opportunity for learning and builds trust in the relationship.

4. *Use review as a way of coaching and mutual learning.* Avoid dictating the causes and solutions, and use questions to promote review and learning. Choose your timing carefully. If you are too immediate after a mistake, the other person(s) may be too emotional or defensive to get the learning from the review. Equally, if you leave it too long the moment will pass and memories will be too dim to accurately record events. As such, learning will diminish. One way around this is to encourage people to keep a note of what worked well and why, and the problems/opportunities for improvement during the work, with a review session scheduled two days after completion of a stage or the whole project.

5. *Plan to coach.* Identify issues and challenges that will provide productive coaching opportunities. Schedule coaching time into your diary.

6. *Use process thinking as your guide.*

Before you start coaching it pays to do some preparation. What is the purpose of the work you want your team member to complete? What

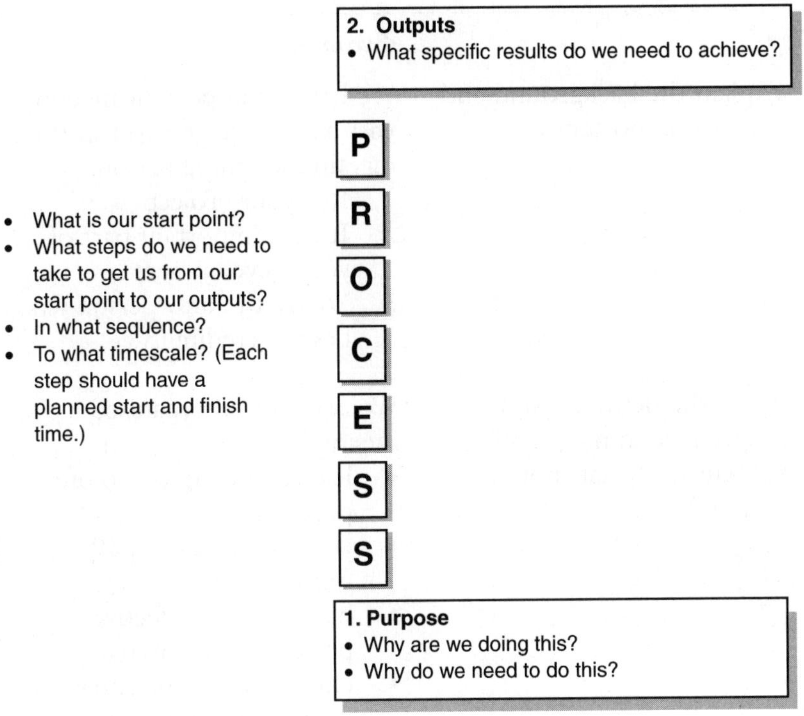

2. Outputs
- What specific results do we need to achieve?

P

R

O

C

E

S

S

- What is our start point?
- What steps do we need to take to get us from our start point to our outputs?
- In what sequence?
- To what timescale? (Each step should have a planned start and finish time.)

1. Purpose
- Why are we doing this?
- Why do we need to do this?

Figure 6.2 Process thinking

are the specific outputs that need to be delivered? What are the key steps in the process? The purpose and outputs help to explain why it is important and what is expected. Thinking through the process gives you a framework to follow in your head. If you feel the team member has missed something important, phrase it as a question rather than a statement whenever possible.

Coaching and the link to delegation

As we have already discussed, two of the main barriers to delegating are the fear of losing control and the concern that no one else has the capability to undertake the task. Coaching provides a solution to both issues. Indeed, coaching should be integrated into the delegation model to increase the chances of success and meaningful development. The framework overleaf illustrates how to do this.

The 'Toolbox' section has a list of coaching questions to help you get started.

Step	Example
1. Explain the background and why it is important.	We have an important meeting with x. I'd like you to run this meeting for three reasons: 1. It is your project. 2. It is an important part of your development. 3. You're the only person who has the credibility.
2. Agree the desired result: • specific and measurable • focus on 'what' not 'how'.	We need a well organised meeting that: • leaves x saying yes to our proposals • lasts no more than 40 minutes • has clear and effective presentation material • enhances your personal credibility and the reputation of our company.
3. Highlight any dangers or pitfalls to be avoided. (Point out what they should avoid.)	Some of the dangers are: • leaving the planning and organisation too late • not preparing well enough • not speaking to each key participant before the meeting.
4. Highlight the resources that are available if required (financial, technical, people).	You can use the boardroom if you want it, and the rest of the team will be asked to help you pull the material together if you need them.
5. Summarise by asking the person to recap.	Are you clear so far? Just give me a recap of what we have covered so far, please.

6. Ask the person how he/she thinks he/she will tackle the job. • Use questions to draw out problems. • Make some suggestions if people are clueless but keep the responsibility with them for thinking it through.	OK, so how do you think you will tackle this? What would be the impact of that? Who would need to be involved? OK, so you are unsure how to plan it. The key is to start at the end and work backwards. When's the meeting? So when must the material be ready? And what needs to happen to get the material ready?
7. Discuss the consequences.	Great – you've got a good approach. What are going to be the benefits of this? What are the consequences of getting it wrong?
8. Agree key milestone meetings.	So I can help. When should we meet to discuss progress?
9. Ask the other person to summarise.	OK, this looks great. Please talk me through a summary of your plan.

Recognition

There is no such whetstone, to sharpen a good wit and encourage a will to learning, as its praise.

Roger Ascham (1515–1568)

I should have praised more.
Duke of Wellington

Recognition is a core element of Timeless Management. It helps to renew people's commitment by building their sense of worth and their self-esteem. It is also essential as a platform for continued

145

learning and growth. In the absence of credible feedback and rewards, people take few risks and slow down on their learning and openness to change.

Recognition causes performance. Where expectations are high and clear and where recognition is plentiful and immediate, people tend to perform. Where expectations and recognition are low or unclear, people tend to perform below their potential.

It is our experience that most people could stand a lot more recognition. We all differ, but there is a need in most of us to feel valued and acknowledged. We benefit from knowing that what we do has meaning, and that we are improving, moving on and avoiding 'going to sleep' in a comfort zone. The recognition can take many forms, from verbal feedback to financial rewards. The important thing is to get it right and to personalise it to the individual; to provide recognition that is suited to them, not to what you prefer.

Effective leaders cause recognition to grow into 'the way we do things around here'. It flows freely. For this to happen, we need to notice what people are doing and provide feedback to them. The kind of things we should be looking to recognise include individual progress, contributions to team effectiveness, impact on you and creative mistakes.

Individual progress

Notice people who achieve something new. The scope is huge. For example: meeting a personal objective, conquering a fear (e.g. presenting to a group), challenging their own traditional patterns of thought or emotions, acting on a value or a new behaviour.

Team effectiveness

Notice people who help the team. For example, people who listen and communicate well, encourage others, invent ideas or options, elevate team morale or standards, reduce tension, help the group to reach agreement, find or share resources, lead or follow appropriately, clarify decisions, help the group to succeed.

Impact on you

Notice people who help or inspire you, especially if the result is to increase your own ability, confidence or satisfaction.

Creative mistakes

Notice people who attempt new actions or behaviours, even if they do not fully succeed, especially if they have a positive impact on you or others: for example: lateral thinking or fresh ideas, low-cost experiments which could result in a breakthrough, attempts from which something valuable is learned, partial solutions or milestones on the way to success.

One of the other key points regarding recognition is the need to give constructive critical feedback as well as praise. The purpose of recognising people is to show your appreciation and to help them to develop. We show our appreciation of others by paying attention to them. Pointing out potential areas for improvement is as valid a way of doing this as praising, provided there is a balance between the two. We help them to learn through two routes:

- highlighting the behaviour that we value, in order to encourage them to do more of it
- highlighting inappropriate behaviour so the individual can choose to improve.

When John works with a team to improve their performance, one of the common requests from team members of their leader is for more constructive critical feedback. The important point here is 'constructive'. It is easy to drain people's enthusiasm with poor quality feedback. Even when we are being critical, it is vital to leave the recipient's self-esteem in good working order. Unfortunately, due to a lack of training, some managers are able to deflate their team members when praising! The process of giving and receiving feedback is one of the most important concepts for inspiring individual growth and developing teamwork. Through feedback, individuals get to know how other people see them, and they can then make different choices about their behaviour. Giving feedback effectively implies certain key ingredients: caring, trusting, acceptance, openness and a concern for the needs of others. Giving and receiving feedback are skills which can be learnt and developed.

The way we receive and deliver feedback is heavily influenced by our thinking. If we see feedback as a way to get things 'off our chest' and make us feel better, we will run a higher risk of antagonising the recipient. If we feel that we have no right to offer feedback, we will never do it. If we believe feedback has to involve an argument, it is likely that it will become exactly that. If we perceive feedback as a threat, we will be defensive. We suggest that a more effective perception of feedback includes:

- Feedback is helpful, it provides information for continuous improvement. When I provide effective feedback I am helping the other person. When I am receiving feedback it is valuable information to help me search for improvements.
- I always have the choice to decide. I can decide to agree with the feedback and act on it. I can decide that there is insufficient trend evidence to merit a change and do nothing.

Effective feedback is built on the foundation of character: values, moral courage, honesty, integrity and graciousness. As each person is different, there is no 'one size fits all' approach. We need to take the time to know and understand each of the people we lead. Indeed, in some ways, this is the very pinnacle of recognition. However, we believe there are a number of principles which, if followed, increase the chances of your feedback being effective.

Ten principles for using praise to build self-esteem and encourage appropriate behaviour

1 Be descriptive not judgmental

Remember way back towards the beginning of this book we talked about everything being a perception? We perceive events and then tend to speak as though this is the only truth. When offering feedback it is important to describe what you observed rather than make an evaluation or judgement. For example, 'I found your report difficult to read. I struggled to find a logical flow of ideas and recommendations' is descriptive of your experience. 'You are clearly poor at writing reports and need to be trained' is evaluative and judgmental. Focusing on describing your own reaction is less inflammatory than making statements of opinion. As such, the other person feels less of a need to respond defensively. The individual is more likely to be open to consider it, and to decide whether to act on it. Focus on what is said and done, not your assumptions about why it might have been said and done. The 'why' takes us from the observable to the inferred. Telling a person what his or her motives or intentions are more often than not tends to alienate the person and contributes to a climate of resentment, suspicion and distrust.

Focus on the behaviour not on the person.

2 Be specific not general

If individuals are to change or improve, they need specific information to understand your perception of their behaviour and the potential consequences of it. To be told that 'You swamped the meeting' is less informative than hearing someone point out that 'You appeared to be speaking for 80 per cent of the time in the meeting. When others made suggestions it looked to me as though you were not really listening to them. As a result, I feel a little concerned that there could be a lack of commitment to the decisions that were taken.'

3 Be helpful

Feedback should be designed to offer help to the other person. It should not be given with the intention of making you feel better.

4 Be 'immediate'

We live in a real world, not a textbook, so being immediate in all our feedback is impractical. However, the principle still holds true. Feedback has the most impact when it is delivered at the earliest opportunity. The other factor to consider here, however, is whether the other person is ready to hear it. If he or she is full of euphoria or despair, he/she is unlikely to be in an appropriate state of mind to listen effectively, and to truly consider learning from it.

5 Be sensitive to the recipient's feedback preferences

Some people have a thirst for feedback, others find it very difficult to receive. Some like a 'round the houses' approach, others prefer it 'straight between the eyes'. As our objective is to help other people, we need to tailor our feedback to meet their needs. They are our customers. To be able to tailor our approach, we need to know them.

6 Ask rather than impose

Feedback is usually best received when the recipient actively seeks it. He or she will be interested and open to it. Clearly there will be times when you want to provide feedback when the other person has not requested it. In these circumstances it usually helps to ask permission before launching in. 'I have some observations, would you like to hear them?' seems to work well.

7 *Refer only to behaviour the recipient can influence*

Commenting on factors that are beyond the person's influence only increases their frustration and annoyance. Often it is the organisation's system that causes unexpected results, not the individual. Equally, comments regarding a person's innate physical or psychological make-up can be both offensive and damaging.

8 *Leave the recipient with the power to choose*

You cannot make other people act on your feedback. It has to be their choice. If they ask for your advice once they have accepted the feedback, then certainly help them. However, at the feedback stage, focus on sharing information rather than giving advice. By sharing information, we leave a person free to decide.

9 *Own the feedback*

Make it clear that these are your perceptions and observations. Avoid hiding behind 'I do not agree but it has been mentioned to me that ...'.

10 *Check their understanding*

Even when our intention is to help, feedback can appear threatening to the recipient. In these circumstances there is the risk of misinterpretation and distortion. Ask the recipient to paraphrase the feedback to check for accuracy.

These principles apply to providing feedback generally. We believe there are some important additional points for providing constructive critical feedback and for effectively receiving feedback. The following steps are suggested as an approach to giving constructive critical feedback:

1. *'Immediately' describe the event in behavioural terms and explain the effect.* Relate clearly in specific, observable and behavioural terms the nature of the behaviour and the effect of it on you,

the work group or the organisation. If you can appropriately say something to reduce the employee's embarrassment, the employee is more likely to accept the feedback non-defensively.

2. *Ask what happened.* Before assuming that the person is at fault, ask what happened. In many instances, the process not the person can be the cause. Equally, the individual may only be partially responsible. Give the recipient an opportunity to explain before you proceed; you may receive information that will prevent you from angering the individual and embarrassing you.

3. *Help the person to accept the need for improvement.* The more time spent in step 2 (finding out what happened), the easier step 3 will be. The person needs to learn from the experience in order to reduce the probability of a recurrence. Unless this step is handled effectively, the person will see himself or herself as a victim, rather than as someone who made a mistake and is willing to correct it. This requires you to be motivated by improvement rather than anger and recrimination.

4. *Focus on the future.* Once the person has chosen to take responsibility for improving, the next step is to help him or her. This is the point to start the coaching process. Our aim is to develop a plan to prevent a recurrence.

5. *Reaffirm your confidence in the individual.* This feedback is addressing just one aspect of the person's performance. We need to avoid a downward spiral of 'I'm no good'. Ask the person how he or she feels about the situation. If necessary, reassure him or her of the quality of the plan for the future. Agree milestone review dates to reflect on progress. Most of all, allow the person to see that you are not judging him or her, that you still value the person as a person. If you are dealing with someone who is consistently under-performing, you may need to take a more assertive approach.

To gain the most we can from the feedback others give us, we need to see it as an opportunity not a threat. This can be a challenge, especially if the individual giving the feedback has not been trained in the skill of it. Equally, some people may not have help on their mind. They may want to 'have a go' in an attempt to make themselves feel better. If we see feedback as a threat, we are likely to be defensive. If we are defensive with those who are trying to help us, it will dissuade them from doing so in the future. If we are defensive with those who want to 'have a go', we are likely to have an argument! In both circumstances we reduce our opportunity to learn and improve. There is no reason why we should accept abusive or aggressive behaviour from others. However, we do have a choice in how we respond. The following guide to effectively receiving feedback may help.

1. *Look on all feedback as helpful.*
2. *Listen to understand before you say anything.*
3. *Summarise to test your understanding.*
4. *Ask for examples.* If the person giving feedback is unable to provide any, he or she might be 'having a go' rather than trying to be constructive.
5. *Thank the individual.* This reassures him or her that the relationship is still intact. It also signals that you value the courage and effort he or she has shown in providing the feedback, and that you are open to it. As such this increases the opportunity for feedback from that person in the future.
6. *Think about the feedback.* Does it strike a chord with you? Have you had similar feedback before? Is a trend emerging or is it an isolated incident? What are the consequences of doing nothing? What could be gained by changing? What are the risks?
7. *Decide whether to act.* If you decide not to act, remember the feedback in case you get anything similar in the future. If you do decide to act:
8. *Develop a plan.* What do you need to do differently? What are the causes? What solutions are available? Who could help you? What are the steps, in what order, by when?

Recognition is a key leadership skill. It is also a central skill to effective parenting. Do we wait for a young child to speak or walk perfectly before praising them? No, we make a fuss, delighted at the progress they have made, reinforcing that their behaviour is in the right direction. Why are we less supportive when dealing with fellow adults? Our need for recognition is with us for life, not just for childhood.

Review

> Wise men appreciate all men, for they see the good in each
> And know how hard it is to make anything good.
>
> Gracián, 1647

Recognition needs to be 'immediate'. Review is planned. Mutual review is another form of recognition. It stresses partnership and a focus on continuous improvement. There are two aspects to review: the review of how particular projects or jobs are progressing, and a general review of how an individual is developing. We have already explored the review of projects or jobs during the 'Measurement, planning and review' section of 'Focus'. Here, we want to explore the importance of making time to discuss how you and your team members feel about progress. This choice to periodically take time out to discuss how individuals feel about their role, their performance, their aspirations and the relationship with you and others is an important demonstration that you value them. However, as with everything, to be successful it needs to be approached with the correct thinking and appropriate behaviour.

We believe that the common approach to review is wrong. As in many aspects of life, the language used gives a clue to the underlying thinking. 'Appraisal' suggests a focus on judgement: 'I will appraise you on how you have done.' Not very mutual, is it? Within this bubble of judgement, the focus often gravitates to what the individual has failed to do, with little emphasis on recognising a person's strengths and achievements. The appraiser spends more time talking than listening, and appears interested only in achieving what is important to him or her. Not very mutual, and not very inspiring.

How does this situation arise? Clearly there will be a multitude of causes, and each organisation will have its own contributing circumstances. However, we believe that the following hypothesis has validity. First of all, the more instinctive focus for most managers is to complete tasks. This is reinforced by the organisation, as its managers usually ask about the progress of tasks, and pay and reward policies are focused on compensating people for the achievement of tasks. As organisations consider this, there is a realisation that some aspect of measurement of whether an individual is performing is needed. Otherwise, how do we know who is worth more than someone else? Similarly, some organisations wake up to realise that while the achievement of tasks is critical to success, it is an output, a result. The road to achieving tasks is paved by enthusiastic and able people. As managers are usually preoccupied with the achievement of tasks, they spend little time valuing people. To counter this, the organisation introduces an 'appraisal scheme' to push managers to make time to value people. However, as the underlying thinking of the managers has not changed, this is resented because it takes time away from achieving tasks. It is seen as a useless bureaucratic exercise. This leads to the following things:

- The focus is on judgmental review; blame appears more important than improvement.
- Employees are compared with each other.
- The energy goes into providing a numerical rating of performance, often at the expense of discussion.
- Review meetings are avoided, cancelled or repeatedly postponed because 'something important has cropped up'.
- Feedback is saved up until the annual review meeting.
- The purpose of the exercise is seen as completing the paperwork on time.
- The same approach is taken with everyone, with little thought about how best to tailor the meeting to meet the needs of the individual.

In turn, the combination of these factors can lead to some very unhelpful consequences. A focus on judgement and blame breeds resentment. It creates a distance in the relationship, implying a teacher–pupil environment. It feeds mistrust, as most managers are rarely in a position to assess day to day performance accurately. Comparing employees with each other corrodes teamwork, as people begin to compete with their team members, focusing on looking good as individuals. Because appropriate measures and feedback mechanisms are absent in the work processes, and there is an absence of measurable objectives, focusing on a numerical rating is usually subjective. This becomes the main event. A mutual discussion of what went well and why, and what would benefit from improvement and how, is therefore unlikely to take place. This is even more likely if the salary increase or bonus is discussed as part of the review discussion. Rating forms do not focus on behaviour. As the individual may see the rating as subjective and inaccurate, this again is likely to breed resentment.

Delaying and postponing review meetings sends the message that other things are more important than the individual. People are too smart not to notice the priority that is put on things. As such, the validity of the whole process is undermined. When the manager does make the time to hold the review meeting, the other person may already be 'switched off'. Saving up feedback until the review leads to either some nice surprises or nasty shocks. Either way it is too late to feel proud or to learn from the feedback. Guess what: it tends to lead to resentment. Seeing the purpose of the exercise as completing the paperwork and taking the same approach with everyone suggests that the reviewer is 'going through the motions', complying with the guidelines rather than valuing the individual.

To avoid these pitfalls we recommend that your thinking regarding review discussions should be guided by the following principles.

Ten principles for effective review discussions

- *The purpose is to help you and the other person to continue to improve and enjoy your work.*
- *It is a partnership.* The feedback should be two-way. It provides a great opportunity to review the expectations exchange you have agreed. What do you need to do differently to help the other person help you?
- *Make time for the meeting, and keep to the agreement.*
- *It is a conversation which then gets recorded onto a form.* It is not about filling in forms and passing them between you and your team members.
- *It is the end of a process that goes on all the time:* a process between you and your team members which is based on effective communication and regular recognition of achievement and areas for improvement.
- *Both of you should prepare using the same pre-work questions.*
- *The review discussion should start with the team member discussing how he or she feels he/she has done.* By doing this the other person feels that his or her opinion is valuable. It also provides you with an insight into his or her perception. If you talk first there is the risk that the individual will just nod in agreement, or start to disagree with you. Both make the conversation more difficult than it need be. You should be listening actively. If you are, there is a high chance that you will learn from the conversation. Work through the pre-work questions in turn, allowing the other person to go first on each occasion. Listen, check your understanding and then offer your own thoughts.
- *There should be no surprises from you.* Your feedback should be a summary of things you have already discussed. It should never be 'new, old news'.
- *Apply the principles for effective feedback.* We want to preserve and

increase the other person's self-esteem, even when we are giving constructive critical feedback.

- *Tackle the difficult conversations.* Constructive critical feedback is essential for performance improvement. As a manager, you are the custodian of the assets of the organisation. You are obligated to tackle any wasteful and counter-productive activities and behaviours. You also have the right and the authority to ask for improvement where it is needed. However, this right also brings with it the responsibility to assist the other person to work out how to improve.

Fun/humour

If we may believe our logicians, man is distinguished from all other creatures by the faculty of laughter.

Joseph Addison (1672–1719)

He who laughs, lasts
Mary Pettibone Poole, 1938

Without humour you cannot run a sweetie shop, let alone a nation.

John Buchan (1875–1940)

It interests us that in the vast array of writings on management issues, relatively little attention is paid to fun. We spend a large part of our life at work. Fun and humour play a central part in life. It makes life and work more bearable, more enjoyable, and it relieves stress – even at Court. Edward de Vere, Earl of Oxford, had just returned to the Court from seven years' self-imposed exile. He was acutely embarrassed by breaking wind in Queen Elizabeth I's presence. His embarrassment would been have increased by the Queen's retort: 'My lord, I had forgotten the fart!'

Humour helps turn the wheels of achievement and can reduce friction in relationships. In short, it can change the atmosphere for the better. Yet in many places of work you could easily be lead to believe that fun was public enemy number one. Perhaps business in general allows itself to be carried away with a sense of its own importance. Could we be confusing our seriousness of purpose with having to be serious, dour and mean spirited? 'But we are so stressed out!' we hear you cry. And we know it is true, the world of work is increasingly stressful. Competition and expectations are higher than ever. We are expected to continually achieve more with less. But this is our very point: more than ever before we all need to be getting some fun from our work, and our life.

Fun is a difficult quality to define. It is a very personal thing. One person's idea of fun can be a nightmare for someone else. However it is defined, having fun is a key requirement for a satisfying job. Success needs exuberance and intensity of feeling. This is difficult to sustain unless people are enjoying themselves. Intensity of purpose is a voluntary activity. When you are having fun, work can become play.

We believe that you do not have to have a permanent smile on your face to be enjoying yourself and having fun, although being positive and cheerful does help others. Fun at work is when you have meaningful work, in a positive environment and you are working towards something you believe in. However, surveys show that the majority of employees do not have fun at work. Much of this is attributed to a lack of influence over their work. The feeling of being controlled is not most people's idea of fun. Yet the majority of management thinking, the design of jobs and work processes are all rooted in a control mentality. Not much mutuality there then. If you apply the principles in this book, you have the opportunity to consciously design a place of work that is fun.

In his book *Further up the Organisation*, the former head of Avis, Robert Townsend, linked achievement with fun. He wrote, 'If it's not excellent it won't be profitable or fun, and if you're not in business for fun or profit, what the hell are you doing here?'

Even for leaders in adversity, such as Sir Winston Churchill, humour was part of their everyday lives. One of Churchill's biographers, Martin Gilbert, who as part of his research read a large number of files, remarked, 'In almost every file there was something to make me laugh.'

Humour can be used to remind people of what is important, it can defuse difficult situations, and it helps to nurture relationships. The use of humour between strangers is a way to break down barriers. This helps you to do business faster. It can be used to put people at ease and reduce their inhibitions, so you get to find out more of what people really think. It can also encourage people to examine their own thinking, without you having to be too direct. Humour can help to lower resistance. There is one qualification here: the humour has to be appropriate. It can easily be misinterpreted, and it can cause offence. Effective humour is never at someone's expense.

The Iron Duke had a sharp and at times sarcastic sense of humour. This was demonstrated in Vienna when the French marshals, annoyed at their defeat, rudely turned their backs on Wellington. He merely smiled, remarking to a bemused onlooker, 'Madam, I have seen their backs before.'

Heavy sarcasm and put-downs can damage self-esteem and create resentment. We suggest these are avoided at all costs, unless you have discussed and agreed mutually acceptable 'ground rules'.

Apart from the anecdotal evidence, we believe it can be shown that fun, which might as easily result from working productively in a team as having a good laugh, is good for business in a serious way. A range of personal benefits emanate from having fun and the use of humour: reduced stress; disarming of negativity; defusing tension; production of positive attitudes, including the sense of belonging (see Chapter 1); and, increasing the likelihood of developing new ideas and embracing change. As to the knock-on corporate benefits, these include higher morale; reduced staff turnover; reduced absenteeism; and higher productivity. So, not engendering a workplace where people can have fun is no laughing matter.

Mutuality: key points

- High performance relies on commitment. Commitment is a voluntary activity. People have to choose to be committed; you cannot force it, that would be coercion.
- Commitment tends to be sustained only if there is a continued sense of worth and ownership: a sense that the individual is part of something important and worthy, a mutual endeavour with mutual benefits.

Trust and synergy

- Trust reduces the amount of time and energy wasted in suspicion and politics. This time and effort can therefore be better deployed on added-value activities that help to deliver the purpose and vision.
- When trust, competence and alignment come together we can achieve synergy, and unlock high performance.
- To develop into an attuned team the members of the group have to be able to trust each other.

- To develop and sustain trust, our words and actions need to be aligned.
- If we fail to deliver on a promise, or betray a confidence, why should anyone trust us?
- Trust is fostered by you being honest, consistent, realistic, following through and acting fairly and decently, and therefore being trustworthy.
- This is a personal decision, built when you behave with integrity and principle.
- Creation of trust, along with supportive teamwork, is key to restoring morale and enthusiasm to a team, department or organisation.

Win–win

- Win–win is the philosophy of mutual gain. Win–lose is one of rivalry.
- Win–win values relationships and the long term, win–lose is driven by ego and short-term results.
- Over time, win–lose becomes lose–lose. Both parties become focused on damaging the other.
- Huge amounts of energy are wasted in organisations due to unhealthy competition between individuals and departments.

Coaching

- Coaching by an effective manager is the most powerful form of development.
- It is about raising awareness of how the team or individual is performing, stimulating the individual to think about this, and using situations as they arise and effective questions to provide development opportunities.
- The whole process is based on promoting discovery. The objective is to expand the individual's knowledge and experience by provoking thought and sharing your experiences.
- Effective coaching is based on questions.
- Where needed, share your experience, both positive and negative.
- Use review as a way of coaching and mutual learning.

Avoid dictating the causes and solutions, and use questions to promote review and learning.

- Plan to coach. Identify issues and challenges that will provide productive coaching opportunities. Schedule coaching time into your diary.
- Use process thinking as your guide. What is the purpose of the work you want your team member to complete? What are the specific outputs that need to be delivered? What are the key steps in the process?

Recognition

- Recognition renews people's commitment by building their sense of worth and their self-esteem.
- It is also essential as a platform for continued learning and growth.
- In the absence of credible feedback and rewards, people take few risks and slow down on their learning and openness to change.
- Recognition causes performance.
- Effective leaders cause recognition to grow into 'the way we do things around here'. It flows freely.
- For this to happen, we need to notice what people are doing and provide feedback to them.
- The kind of things you should be looking to recognise include individual progress, contributions to team effectiveness, impact on yourself and creative mistakes.
- Effective recognition assists people to learn through two routes: highlighting the behaviour that we value (in order to encourage them to do more of it), and highlighting inappropriate behaviour so the individual can choose to improve.
- Even when we are being critical, it is vital to leave the recipient's self-esteem in good working order.
- The process of giving and receiving feedback is one of the most important concepts for inspiring individual growth and developing teamwork.
- Feedback is helpful, it provides information for continuous improvement. When you provide effective feedback you are helping the other person. When you

receive feedback it is valuable information to help you search for improvements.

- As each person is different, there is no 'one size fits all' approach. Tailor the approach to the person.
- To gain the most we can from the feedback others give us, we need to see it as an opportunity not a threat.
- Recognition is a key leadership skill.

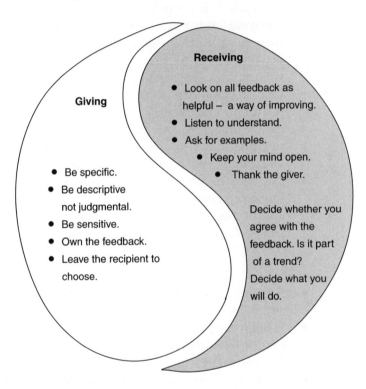

Figure 6.3 Framework for effectively giving and receiving feedback

Review

- Mutual review is another form of recognition. It stresses partnership and a focus on continuous improvement.
- A focus on judgement and blame breeds resentment. It creates a distance in the relationship, implying a teacher–pupil environment.

161

- Most managers are rarely in a position to assess day to day performance accurately.
- Comparing employees with each other corrodes teamwork, as people begin to compete with their team members, focusing on looking good as individuals.
- Rating forms do not focus on behaviour. As the other person may see the rating as subjective and inaccurate, this again is likely to breed resentment.
- Delaying and postponing review meetings sends the message that other things are more important than the person you are to meet with. People are too smart not to notice the priority that is put on things.
- Constructive critical feedback is essential for performance improvement.
- As a manager, you are the custodian of the assets of the organisation. You are obligated to tackle any wasteful and counter-productive activities and behaviours.
- You also have the right and the authority to ask for improvement where it is needed. However, this right also brings with it the responsibility to assist the other person to work out how to improve.

Fun

- Fun makes life and work more bearable, more enjoyable, and relieves stress.
- It helps turn the wheels of achievement and can reduce friction in relationships.
- Success needs exuberance and intensity of feeling.
- Intensity of purpose is a voluntary activity.
- Fun at work is when you have meaningful work, in a positive environment and you are working towards something you believe in.
- Surveys show that the majority of employees do not have fun at work.
- Much of this is attributed to a lack of influence over their work.
- Yet the majority of management thinking, the structure of jobs and the design of work processes are usually rooted in a control mentality.

- The use of humour can help you to do business faster and more effectively.
- Effective humour is never at someone's expense. Heavy sarcasm and put-downs can damage self-esteem and create resentment.
- A range of personal benefits emanate from having fun and the use of humour.
- The corporate benefits include higher morale, reduced staff turnover, reduced absenteeism and higher productivity.
- Not engendering a workplace where people can have fun is no laughing matter.

 ## Mutuality toolbox

Coaching

You may find some of the following questions useful in your coaching discussions.

- What options can you think of?
- What advantages does each option offer?
- What are the risks/disadvantages with each option?
- What would happen if ...?
- What would be the consequences of doing that?
- What would the implications be if we did that?
- What would the impact be if we did that?
- If that happened to you, how would you feel about it?
- If you were in their position what would you want/expect?
- If you were in their position what would be bothering you?
- What are the biggest barriers to success?
- How can we remove these barriers?
- Who would need to be involved?
- Who would need to know?

Recognition

Recognition is one of our fundamental needs; however, unless you know what you want in the first place, you are less likely to find it, or to see spontaneous opportunities to express appreciation. Take a few moments and make some notes for use with your own colleagues and staff.

- What milestones are about to be reached?
- What forms of reward would be meaningful to the people on your team?
- How therefore can you personally show your appreciation to others?

Some suggested ways to show your appreciation

Remember, be descriptive and specific. You need people to understand exactly what you have appreciated.

- Personal face to face thank you.
- Greeting people by name when you pass them in the corridor or go past their place of work.
- Letters from you, your manager, the chief executive.
- Personal phone calls from you, your manager, the chief executive.
- Face to face thank you from your manager, the chief executive.
- Greeting cards.
- Handwritten postcards.
- Write a number of 'post it' notes and hide them in different places on the person's desk/workspace.
- Have a 'Performance notice board' showing progress against the agreed business objectives.
- Articles in company newsletters.
- Longer lunch break.
- A meal.
- Cream cakes.
- Flowers.
- Engraved pen/pencil.
- Time off.
- Book tokens.
- Magazine subscriptions.
- Bottle of wine or champagne.
- Tickets for sporting or other events.
- Gift vouchers
- Weekend trip for the individual and his or her partner.
- Use of an executive company car for a weekend.
- A gift associated with someone's hobby.

Fun

- Start with yourself. People will take a lead from you.

- Smile a lot, it is contagious.
- Support others who want to have fun.
- Let people know that it is absolutely OK for them to enjoy what they are doing and that the sound of laughter is welcome.
- Encourage the working environment to be enjoyable. Work hard to provide decent facilities. Have humorous notices, pictures, etc. around the place.
- Consider the use of music in the workplace to lift the mood a little.
- Work at removing the rules and practices at work that take the fun out of things.
- Be prepared and be willing to laugh at yourself.
- Look for the positive in every situation.
- Include people in the fun, otherwise it becomes divisive.

Timeless Management historic illustrations

Timeless Manager 9: Sir Christopher Wren – mutuality

Sir Christopher Wren (1632–1723). Architect, Professor of Astronomy (Oxford University) and co-founder of the Royal Society.

Connections with Historic Royal Palaces

Wren, the most important architect of his age, was Surveyor of the King's Works from 1669 to 1718 and was responsible for two huge and significant building projects for William and Mary in the last years of the seventeenth century. In 1689 he was commissioned by the monarchs to rebuild Henry VIII's royal lodgings at Hampton Court as new royal apartments in a sumptuous modern style. Wren had originally planned to demolish the whole of the Tudor palace except the Great Hall, but in the end the outer lodgings of the Tudor palace were retained. At the same time as works were getting under way at Hampton Court, William and Mary purchased Nottingham House in Kensington, which they asked Wren to improve and extend for them. He carried out several phases of work for them, and the building, now called Kensington Palace, became their usual place of residence during the winter months.

Wren himself lived at Hampton Court in the later years of his life. From 1708, he leased a house on Hampton Court Green, just opposite the palace, from the Crown. He substantially rebuilt the house and lived here for the rest of his life.

Sir Christopher's connection with the Tower of London was less pleasant. His uncle, Matthew Wren (the Bishop of Ely) was imprisoned in the Tower in 1642. There he remained, without trial and not convicted of any offence, for 18 years.

Historical illustration

As a boy Christopher Wren, the son of the Dean of Windsor, used to play in the grounds of Windsor Castle with the King's son who later became King Charles II. This was the start of Wren's relationship with royalty, which was to stand him in excellent stead in his later years. As a leading architect he needed and won the patronage of royalty. Perhaps it was those early play sessions that taught him the basics of relationship building with future monarchs. Whether or not this was so, during his long lifetime (he lived for 91 years, nearly three times the average life expectancy of the time), he built and developed important relationships with Charles II, James, William and Mary, Queen Anne and George I in the early years of his reign.

These proved to be mutually beneficial connections and real win–win: the monarchs and the country benefiting from some of the greatest architectural design (including St Paul's Cathedral, improvements and alterations to Hampton Court Palace, 56 churches in London, the Sheldonian Library at Oxford University and Trinity Library at Cambridge University); and Christopher Wren receiving in turn wealth, a knighthood and public approbation. This acclaim was not just limited to his lifetime: even now many would argue that he is still the greatest-ever British architect.

He did not begin his career as an architect. As a boy Wren's real interest was science. By the age of 17 he had already made a number of credible inventions including a weather clock, a pneumatic engine and even a new deaf and dumb language. It was at this age in 1649 that Wren went up to Oxford, to Wadham College. The young Wren excelled at his studies and he eventually became a Fellow of All Souls (1653–61), a sort of professional thinker and academic. He developed a reputation as a brilliant scientist, becoming Professor of Astronomy at Gresham College (1657–61) and Savilian Professor of Astronomy at Oxford University (1661–73).

While at Oxford University, Christopher Wren undertook important research work on a wide range of topics varying from intravenous injections to the theory of motion. Unusually, although he was a leading scientist he published almost nothing. His interest seemed to be in starting ideas off, developing them to an advanced stage and then leaving them for others to finish. There are no definitive explanations for this behaviour, particularly since he was considered to be quite ambitious.

One point his contemporaries appear to agree on is his indifference to his reputation and to taking credit for his work. Thomas Sprat, the Bishop of Rochester and Dean of Westminster Abbey, wrote that Wren 'is so far from usurping the fame of other men, that he endeavours with all care to conceal his own'. In a coincidental crossover and cross-reference between two of our featured Timeless Managers, Isaac Newton pointed out that in the earlier research Wren had carried out on the laws of motion, he had been of tremendous help to Newton. This all seems to suggest that Wren was deeply and sincerely interested in sharing knowledge with other scientists for public rather than personal benefit.

Wren was a leading member of the philosophical club in Oxford. It was following a lecture he gave at Gresham College in late 1660 that Wren and a number of other scientists decided to convert that informal club into what eventually became the Royal Society. It was at first known as the College for the Promoting of Physico-Mathematical Experimental Learning. In 1663 under a second Royal Charter the college became the Royal Society of London for Improving Natural Knowledge. Mutuality was a core reason for the establishment of the Royal Society: for leading scientists to share their knowledge and understanding for the advancement of science and to benefit society. In early 1662 Wren reinforced this view when he set out what he considered the twin roles of the Society were 'from the Converse and Communication of everyone's thoughts', and he believed it should function in a pragmatic way in order to benefit mankind. Wren considered that the 'idea' on its own was insufficient and that the only true test of human cognition and philosophical principles was in their practical result. This is of course a laudable aim, although a little at odds with Wren the scientist, who rarely concluded his own research work. Apart from being a founder member of the Society, he was its President between 1680 and 1682.

Wren's interest in architecture was kindled as a student when he read *On Architecture*, a book written in the first century AD by a Roman architect called Vitruvius. He was also influenced, no doubt, by other members of the Royal Society who had been flirting with architecture. There was an obvious link between the two disciplines: a sound knowledge of mathematics was required by architects. Wren cut his teeth on a new chapel for Pembroke Hall, Cambridge, commissioned by his uncle, followed by the Sheldonian Theatre at Oxford. For a short while his scientific and architectural interests co-existed.

In 1665 Wren left England, some might say at least partly to flee the plague (which eventually killed some 100,000 people) on what turned out to be a seven-month visit to France. Here he met numerous colleagues from science and architecture, and continued internationally the mutual sharing activities of the Royal Society. Importantly Wren was introduced to a different style of architecture, one that was to influence him in his later work. He was particularly interested in and fascinated by the number of domed buildings in Paris compared with England where there were none. Shortly after his return to England in 1666 he was to start work on what was to become one of the world's finest domed buildings, St Paul's Cathedral.

As during his period as a professional academic and scientist, Wren the architect worked with a large number of associates and assistants. He worked in a collaborative way and entrusted his people not just to deal with the detailed work but actually to become involved in the design process proper. One such assistant was the talented architect Nicholas Hawksmoor who worked with Wren in the 1680s and 1690s and built his own reputation as a leading architect: another example of a mutually beneficial almost symbiotic relationship.

The sociable manner in which Wren did business was caricatured some years after his death by Edmund 'Clerihew' Bentley, the originator of a type of poem which he called 'a sort of formless four line verse', which became known as the Clerihew (George III was also 'Clerihewed'):

> Sir Christopher Wren
> Said, 'I am going to dine with some men,
> If anyone calls,
> Say I'm designing St Paul's.'

Wren would also take great pleasure while visiting St Paul's during its construction period to stop and respond to any questions from the ordinary people who visited.

Throughout his long life Sir Christopher Wren spent time in the coffee houses as well as lecture and committee rooms, always eager to share and pass on his considerable knowledge and ideas and develop relationships with people. He was described by a Frenchman, de Monconys, who visited Oxford in 1663, as 'one of the most courteous and most open men that I have found in England'. No doubt this accounted for some enduring friendships, for example with fellow Royal Society member and eminent chemist and physicist, Robert Hooke.

Timeless Manager 10: King Charles II – fun!

King Charles II (1630–1685). King of England, Scotland and Ireland, 1660–85.

Connections with Historic Royal Palaces

For his whole reign, Charles II lived principally at the great palace of Whitehall. Here, in the Banqueting House, he received the many lavish embassies sent to congratulate him on his restoration to the throne, presided at court lotteries and dined with the Knights of the Garter in their annual feast. Also in the Banqueting House, Charles II performed the ancient ceremony known as 'touching for the King's Evil', in which the sovereign touched sufferers from the skin disease scrofula and was supposed to heal them miraculously. From the very beginning of his reign, he performed the ceremony as often as once a week, for example in early July 1660 when the newspaper *Mercuricus Publicus* reported: 'The Kingdom having for a long time, by reason of his Majesties absence, been troubled with the Evil, great numbers have lately flocked for cure. His Sacred Majesty on Monday last touched Two hundred and fifty in the Banqueting-house.'

Charles II also frequently visited his ancient fortress of the Tower of London. On 22 April 1660, the eve of his coronation, the King travelled at dawn to the Tower of London to set out on his extraordinary coronation procession from the Tower to Westminster, and was the last monarch ever to do so.

Historical illustration

It would have been difficult to predict that this son of a decapitated monarch, who spent nine miserable, frustrating and humiliating years in exile, after eventually being restored to the throne in 1660 would be given the sobriquet of 'the Merry Monarch'.

It was the personality of Charles II, which was so different from that of his father, a shy and quiet man of refined tastes, that led to the nickname. Charles II actually sought events and occasions when he could meet and talk to a wide range of people of all backgrounds, and he had a great sense of humour. This approach, which effortlessly put him at ease, was of appeal to his subjects and accounted in large measure for his popularity. Apparently he had the ability to be able to use humour and at the same time not undermine his dignity and position as sovereign, as described by one of his subjects:

> No prince was ever so diverting and amusing as the King.... So affable, that in the galleries and park he would pull off his hat to the meanest; gave great liberties to others in discourse and as he was so affable on one hand, he could take majesty on the other, and I believe was the first and last King that could have his bedchamber door open ... men of assurance and of buffooning humour made the King wink often at their forwardness because they made him laugh for the present, yet when he would he could keep up majesty to the height of his great countenance.

Even as a boy his sardonic style was evident. His mother, Queen Henrietta Maria, wrote to her son threatening to tell Lord Newcastle, his Governor, that he would not take 'physick'. The response of Charles was in a pre-emptory letter to Lord Newcastle when he wrote, 'My Lord, I would not have you take too much physick, for it doth always make me worse and I think it will do the like with you.'

Years later, following his father's beheading, Charles was at the Battle of Worcester where he showed considerable courage. During the battle 2,000 Royalist soldiers were killed compared with about 200 on the Roundhead side. Following his defeat he was convinced to escape England and became a fugitive, hounded by the Parliamentary forces. He was forced to adopt a disguise and spent six dangerous and frightening weeks on the run, hiding in a succession of properties belonging to his supporters.

During this period of obvious strain and tension one of his countless and more comfortable places of refuge was Trent Manor. The Manor was located next to the village church. When the bells rang out unexpectedly the heavily disguised Charles went to find out why, and was told that it was because of the good news that the King was dead. The King's wry response was, 'Alas, poor people!'

This wry sense of humour did not depart Charles in exile. In a letter to Elizabeth Bohemian, one of his aunts, he wrote that there were only two things he needed: fiddlers and someone to teach the new dances. His return to England in 1660 was marked by great rejoicing and celebrations. His sense of humour did not desert him. To a small gathering he quipped that it was his fault that he had been in exile so long because there was no one he had met who 'did not protest that he had ever wished for his return'.

There is some conjecture that the image of the Merry Monarch concealed a darker, more melancholy side, brought on by some dreadful experiences such as his father's death and his period in impecunious exile. Nevertheless, throughout his life the spirit of his secure, happy and carefree childhood, which perhaps had prepared him for the arduous years ahead, resurfaced in humour and wit time and again.

In March 1660 King Charles's humour surfaced in a letter to George Manck, when he wrote, 'And whatever you have heard to the contrary you will find to be as false as if you had been told that I have white hair and I am crooked.' Just over a year after this letter, the coronation of King Charles II took place on 23 April 1661. It was a long day for Charles; beginning at 8.00 am at Tower Hill with a procession through London to Westminster Abbey. His clothing was extremely elaborate, made of cloth of gold, crimson satin and ermine. The solemn ceremony itself was followed by a sumptuous feast in Westminster Hall. Given the solemnity and importance of the occasion it could have been expected that the coronation robes of the new monarch would have been kept in a museum or preserved in some way, but even at such a time the self-mocking humour of Charles came to the fore. He gave them to be used at the theatre, and they were subsequently worn in plays.

In 1673 an Act of Parliament called a Test Act was passed by the Commons. This Act required all holders of high office to take public communion and effectively to demonstrate that they were not Catholics. The King had no alternative but to grant assent on 29 March. Charles II was to use humour to demonstrate the pointlessness of this measure. He vowed to purge his Court of all Catholics except his barber who 'despite his bills' he wanted to keep 'for he was so well accustomed to his hand'. In this remark he was stating that if he could trust a Catholic to be near him with an open razor, then other Catholics hardly presented a threat.

An exchange with Clarendon on a proposed visit to Tunbridge could almost be part of a modern comic double act:

Clarendon: I suppose you will go with a light Train.
King: I intend to take nothing but my night bag.
Clarendon: Yes, you will not go without your horse.
King: I could make that part of my night bag.

All that is missing at the end is 'boom boom'.

Of course, King Charles II was known for his infidelity and his love of women (which arguably perversely increased the standing of women of the time). He sired at least 12 children out of wedlock including two by perhaps his most famous mistress, Nell Gwynn. The Duke of Buckingham is quoted as saying, 'A King is supposed to be the Father of his People, and Charles II was certainly the father of a good many of them.' But Charles did not take such comments to heart. Much later in his reign Thomas Ken, the Bishop of Winchester, refused to allow Nell Gwynn to share with Charles the lodging he had provided. Later Charles could have taken his revenge when Thomas Ken needed his sovereign's approval to move to become the Bishop of Bath and Wells. But Charles did not bear grudges: he readily approved the appointment, adding: 'God's fish! The little black fellow who would not give poor Nelly a night's lodging.'

Rather prematurely John Wilmet, Earl of Rochester, wrote this epitaph-like poem about his King:

Here lies our mutton-eating King,
Whose word no man relies in,
Who never said a foolish thing
Nor ever did a wise one!

Not for the first time King Charles had the last word by responding, 'True, for my words are my own, my actions are my Ministers!' And his humour stayed with him until the very end of his life. He was taken seriously ill on the evening of 1 February 1685 and died some five days later aged 55. In that intervening five days he suffered all the horrors and agonies that 12 seventeenth-century doctors could bestow. Any human today suffering the bleeding, hot irons and awful concoctions then considered medicine would be straight on to Amnesty International, claiming torture. He undoubtedly suffered more at the hands of his doctors than from his illness (which has still not been diagnosed). Despite the pain and anguish during this process, on being told at one stage that he should not speak, he remarked that such an instruction would have killed Harry Killigrew (an infamous chatterbox) but he agreed to comply.

According to Lord Macaulay in his book *History of England* (1849), even the final sentiments of Charles II were humorous: 'He had been, he said, an unconscionable time dying; but he hoped they would excuse it.'

Part III

Timeless Management in the twenty-first century: practising what we preach

A man may be very sincere in good principles, without having a good practice.

Samuel Johnson, 1773

Beginning reform is beginning revolution.

Duke of Wellington (1769–1852)

7 Introduction to Part III

The setting for our case study is Historic Royal Palaces, an organisation operating in the charity or non-profit sector. As previously stated, we do not consider the messages from this book are applicable just to this sector. We believe they are as relevant to the individual or to public or private sector managers wishing to improve their effectiveness in getting things done through people.

However we should not underestimate the importance to UK society of non-profit sector organisations such as Historic Royal Palaces, now and in the future. According to Professor Peter Drucker, writing in *Managing the Non-profit Organisation* about the US experience:

> Today, we know that the non-profit institutions are central to American society and are indeed its most distinguishing feature. We now know that the ability of government to perform social tasks is very limited indeed. But we also know that the non-profits discharge a much bigger job than taking care of specific needs. With every second adult serving as a volunteer in the non-profit sector and spending at least three hours a week in non-profit work, the non-profits are America's largest 'employer'. But they also exemplify and fulfil the fundamental American commitment to responsible citizenship in the community. We now realise that it (the non-profit organisation) is central to the quality of life in America, central to citizenship, and indeed carries the values of American society and of the American tradition.

He continues, 'the non-profit institution has been America's resounding success in the last forty years. In many ways it is the "growth industry" of America.' Whether the non-profit sector in Britain will ever be viewed in this way is a subject for conjecture. We hope it will be, and that in our own small way we will influence the view of the sector by sharing our experiences at Historic Royal Palaces, as well as the thinking behind our Timeless Management concept.

The five palaces

The palaces are described briefly below in order to set the context for the case study.

Historic Royal Palaces is the body responsible for the care, conservation and presentation of the Tower of London, Hampton Court Palace, Kensington Palace State Apartments, the Banqueting House in Whitehall, and Kew Palace with Queen Charlotte's Cottage. The palaces are owned by the Queen on behalf of the nation.

HM Tower of London

The Royal Palace and Fortress of the Tower of London, founded by William the Conqueror in 1066–7, and enlarged and modified by successive sovereigns, is one of the most famous and spectacular fortresses in the world. Enriched by its many living traditions, including its Yeoman Body and the Crown Jewels, the Royal Armouries' displays and other recent improvements, the Tower is today the most visited historic site in Britain. It is a World Heritage site.

Hampton Court Palace

Hampton Court became a royal palace in the 1520s, on its acquisition by Henry VIII from Cardinal Wolsey. Its Tudor buildings are among the most important in existence and William and Mary's improvements an outstanding example of the English baroque. The interiors feature a magnificent collection of pictures and tapestries, largely belonging to the Royal Collection. The buildings are surrounded by 60 acres of garden and 800 acres of royal parkland.

Kensington Palace

Kensington became a royal residence in 1689 with the purchase of an existing house by William and Mary from Sir George Coppin (no relation to one of the authors). Immediately enlarged for them by Christopher Wren, and subsequently altered under George I, the State Apartments contain important interiors by William Kent, many major works of art from the Royal Collection and the Royal Ceremonial Dress Collection.

The Palace was the home of the late Diana, Princess of Wales and the Crowther Gates the unusual focus for national grief, with the massive numbers of floral tributes left there following her tragic death.

Banqueting House, Whitehall

The Banqueting House at Whitehall, designed by Inigo Jones and finished for James I in 1622, is the only remaining complete building of Whitehall Palace, once the kingdom's largest, to have survived the fire of 1698. Immensely significant as the first English building in the Palladian style, it is also famous for its ceiling, painted by Peter Paul Rubens in 1630–4.

Kew Palace

Built as a private house in 1631, Kew Palace, also known as the Dutch House, was used by the Royal Family between 1729 and 1818. In turn with the series of other buildings which once stood nearby, it served as lodgings for servants, as a schoolroom for three generations of royal children, as George III's retreat and as a home for King George, Queen Charlotte and their family.

8 The Timeless Management approach in the Historic Royal Palaces

In 1258 Sa'di, the Persian writer and poet, said, 'A theorist without practice is like a tree without fruit.' We agree. In this and the following chapter we set out how the Timeless Management approach outlined in Parts I and II of this book has been applied in practice. We have not the space here to provide a detailed account but we have attempted to identify the important milestones, particularly in relation to people development, and importantly, to pick out some measures of progress.

The latest management episode in the palaces' lay history began in the last few years of the twentieth century when Historic Royal Palaces was born and partially freed from the government. The organisation ceased being an Executive Agency within the Department for Culture, Media and Sport on 31 March 1998. On 1 April 1998 it entered into a contractual relationship with the Secretary of State to exercise his legal responsibilities with respect to the palaces. Unusually and, as far as we are aware, uniquely among its international peer group of world heritage standard historic sites, under this contract the palaces were established as a charitable trust with no ongoing public funding or revenue subsidy.

In corporate terms Historic Royal Palaces, with a turnover of about £40 million p.a., is small. In the charity sector it is in the 'Footsie 100' of the 188,000 charities registered in England and Wales. And in the cultural/conservation charity sub-sector it is third in the league after the National Trust and British Museum but ahead of organisations such as the British Library, Tate Gallery, English Heritage, the Royal Opera House, the Victoria & Albert Museum and the National Gallery in terms of income generated exclusive of public funding.

Here was an organisation set up as a charity and left to compete in a busy marketplace, and therefore forced to adopt best practice private sector business techniques. Not quite politically correct because of the words 'Royal' and 'Palaces' in its title, the organisation has been a real example, albeit in microcosm, of the prime ministerial ambition to modernise government. Because the link with government was not completely cut, Historic Royal Palaces was to remain a non-departmental public body. In the early days of the new charity it faced another government legacy: ten years' operation of a civil service culture. Alan quickly identified that culture change was essential. A more entrepreneurial approach had to be introduced, without any loss of status and dignity.

Of course change is a constant. The seventeenth-century poet John Milton put this most eloquently when he wrote:

> Since 'tis nature's law to change,
> Constancy, alone, is strange.

With or without Alan's direct interventions numerous changes would have occurred within the palaces, but undoubtedly at a slower rate and in a less managed way.

What we have done in the next part of the book is to select just five of the hundreds of changes that have been introduced since September 1999. Most of the changes that have been implemented have not required Alan's direct involvement; the five we have chosen did. They are:

- the listening exercise
- relationship fixing
- developing the strategic plan
- implementing the plan
- resolving organisation structure anomalies.

The listening exercise

As alluded to in Chapter 6 of this book, listening must be one of the most underrated and little used of management tools. And yet it is so comparatively easy to do! Percy Barnevik, one of the great European business leaders of the late twentieth century, used the listening approach in managing ABB Asea Brown Boveri. He spent a great deal of his time visiting his company's operations which were located in 140 countries. He estimated he listened and spoke to 5,000 of his staff each year.

Before he started working at Historic Royal Palaces Alan understood that, because of his private sector background, he might be perceived as a totally 'commercial' person and this might be seen to be in conflict with the organisation's curatorial aims. So he wanted to give the people a chance to see the whites of his eyes, as well as being able to see the whites of theirs.

Before he started working at the palaces officially, he held individual sessions with members of the Executive Board and Trustees, but it was important to go deeper into the soul of the institution. On joining the organisation he set up a series of meetings with staff: the listening exercise. This activity took over four weeks to complete, in which time Alan did very little office work. He visited all the palaces and held intense sessions with 356 colleagues, sometimes one on one, at other times in groups of three or four, occasionally with as many as nine or ten colleagues.

When he told the Executive Board what he was doing, one of the Executive Directors said, 'This listening exercise is all very well, but the problem is that you have to do something about it.' Exactly! The results of the listening exercise included:

- In some cases, probably the majority, it was a total surprise that the Chief Executive should visit them and was interested in their views.
- There was no shared sense of purpose or vision for the organisation.
- There was no consistent performance management system.
- There was no strategic long-term plan for success.
- There was little or no management or team training.
- Antipathy was expressed towards the personnel department.
- There were organisation structure anomalies.
- There were poor communication processes.
- There was a culture of slow decision making, overwhelming bureaucracy, little listening from directors/managers and lack of staff involvement.

This is quite a comprehensive list but it is only the tip of the iceberg: there were literally hundreds of smaller points that were made, some capable of instant fixes. This may seem a negative exercise but for Alan it was the reverse: it showed there was a job to be done and pointed to some initial priorities for action.

In addition to the practical pointers of items that needed to be fixed, the exercise also gave an impression of the people, and that there was a real pride amongst colleagues in belonging to their palace and a tremendous underlying spirit. There was generally an openness, a 'look you in the eye' attitude and a willingness and readiness to become involved and contribute more. There was also a real aspiration that they wanted to be the best in their area of operations, and not just the best in England but in the world. He concluded the organisation was gagging for a change programme.

The listening exercise influenced all the thinking that followed. Once the exercise had been completed Alan fed back the key messages in personal letters to all staff, and in presentations to Trustees, to Executive Directors and worked with Executive Directors to prepare an action programme for the organisation. This plan started with fixing some of the short-term issues in order to have some quick wins, while the Executive Board prepared a five-year strategic plan.

Relationship fixing

From the listening meetings he attended before he started at Historic Royal Palaces, Alan discovered that two key relationships were not what they should be: between the CEO/Executive Team and Trustees, and between the organisation and the Department for Culture, Media and Sport (DCMS). It was clear that the organisation would not have the freedom to operate unless these relationships were put on a different footing.

An analysis of the root cause of the problems indicated there was an issue of trust. Rightly or wrongly there was a perception that information was being kept from both bodies by the Executive, who wanted to plough their own furrow. Given that to Alan perception is reality, he decided to try to change this view and to do this mainly himself. He thought he would have the greatest equity with the two bodies as the new boy on the block.

Trust takes a long time to establish and it is a two-way process. Alan's style was to be totally open and very direct to Trustees and to the DCMS: he kept nothing from either and significantly upgraded the communication process. With Trustees he instigated a pairing system with Executive Directors to open communication lines. (Initially this did not work because of the hangover from the past.) He provided detailed written 'warts and all' reports every month (Trustees only meet bi-monthly), and he spent time on the phone and meeting a number of Trustees. That process is ongoing.

With the DCMS he adopted the same type of approach, although on a lower scale. He was equally open and gave both bodies the same information.

Given the core importance of staff to the management of Historic

Royal Palaces it was necessary to review relationships with the organisations representing a proportion of the staff: the unions. In 1999 this relationship was rather formal, based on a 'Whitley Council', civil service meeting approach. Although regular meetings were held they were a throwback to the 1930s and 1940s. Management were seated on one side of the huge table and trade union officials and representatives on the other.

The previous 'management' stance to the relationship was also embedded in the earlier part of the twentieth century. There was a closed attitude and certainly no real willingness to share information and work collaboratively together. When the whole new philosophy of the organisation was 'there is no they, only us', it was inconceivable that this style of relationship could continue. So a concerted attempt was made by Graham Josephs, the Personnel and Development Director of Historic Royal Palaces, to review and improve the formal union mechanisms to reflect a more modern partnership approach. This new way of working was also in complete accord with one of the seven strategic goals (set out later in this chapter), to develop mutually beneficial relationships with partners. There was a need for the union officials and representatives to feel involved and wanted.

The response of the union people to the new open style was immediate and positive. Extremely effective meetings were arranged along with half-day interactive workshops, not just for Graham and Alan to present and explain issues but, more importantly, for them to listen and to learn. Union officials had a wealth of experience and contacts which could be tapped for mutual benefit.

Although it is relatively early days, all of these relationships with key interested parties seem to have grown considerably stronger over time. The real test is that Alan and his team have had the authority to introduce some sweeping changes with the total support of the Trustees, the DCMS and the unions.

Developing the Strategic Plan

Informed by the listening exercise, the next step was to involve Executive Directors and managers in developing the direction of the organisation. Executive Directors for the first time spent time together off-site in intense facilitated sessions. The methodology adopted is set out in Figure 8.1.

The first step was to define the draft purpose and vision statements, which were then refined to become:

185

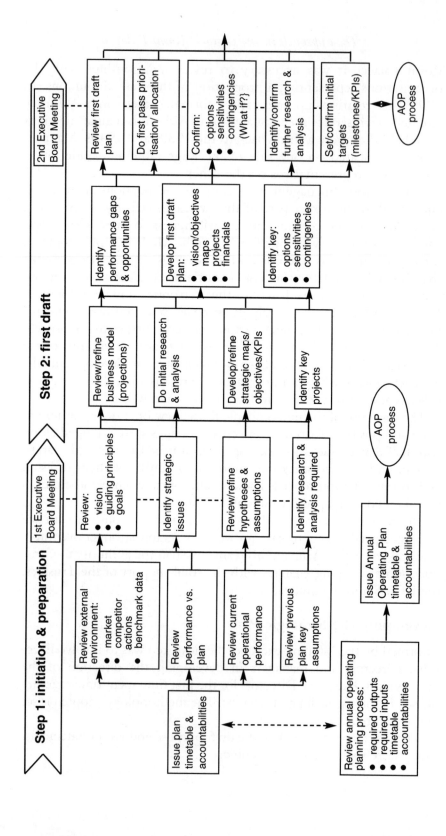

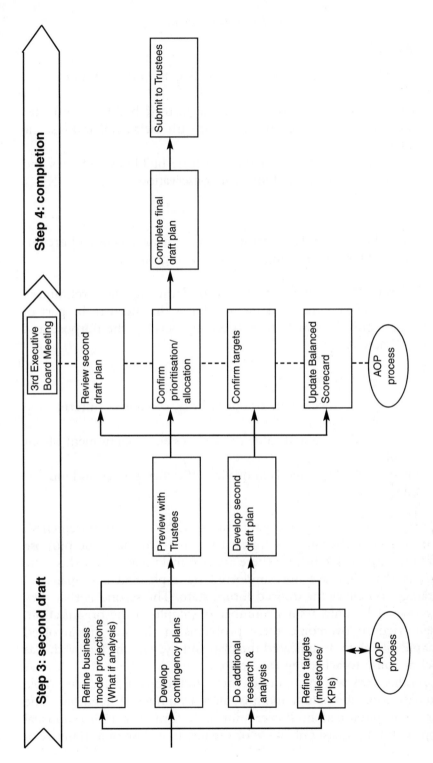

Figure 8.1 HRP Strategic Planning Process

Our purpose

As defined in the Royal Charter, for the benefit of the nation to:

- Manage, conserve and improve the historic buildings and sites in our care to a standard consistent with their royal and historic status.
- Educate the public about these historic buildings and sites and about the skills required for their conservation.

Our vision

> We will be the world-leader in the care, management and presentation of historic buildings, contents and grounds.

Time and effort were also put into deducing the preliminary guiding principles, the fundamental things that need to be part of the organisation's culture to successfully develop the purpose and vision. These are:

Our guiding principles

- Exceed the expectations of our visitors, customers (internal and external) and partners.
- Invest in, develop and value the abilities and commitment of our people.
- Pursue the highest levels of quality, efficiency, service and innovation.

We are aware of many organisations with 'mission statements'. Unfortunately they do not appear to be used to their true purpose and full impact. We believe there are two main reasons for this. The first is that they are not supported by a planned and managed strategy to deliver the desired future state. The second is that they are owned by only a small number of people in the organisation. Alan tried to overcome these problems in the way he involved people in and communicated the plan and by, what he believed, was a clear route to achieving the desired aims.

All this work was incorporated into a full five-year plan. The whole exercise took about four months, after a number of iterations. The plan was published in PowerPoint slide format, a rather unusual approach for a quasi public sector organisation. Use of a number of the traits such as simplicity and clarity shaped the plan and its presentation which are summarised in Figures 8.2, 8.3 and 8.4.

Figure 8.2 summarises a Porter's Five Forces analysis undertaken in 2000. It shows on the one hand a highly competitive and saturated visitor attraction marketplace, exacerbated by new attractions subsidised by the Lottery. On the other, Historic Royal Palaces is seen to benefit from owning established properties of scale, with prime locations in the South-East of England feeding off the affluent Greater London area. Nevertheless, in 2000 even before the impact of foot and mouth disease and the 11 September atrocities, the critical overseas market was affected by the strength of the pound.

The vision statement inspired by staff is at the top of the pyramid in Figure 8.3. The gaps in capability were assessed by using the business excellence model (BEM). This showed the organisation scoring modestly against the BEM enablers and slightly better against the elements underpinning excellent results. The use of the BEM framework validated the views formed during the listening exercise. A change to a performance management culture was necessary.

Another area of concern was the heavy reliance on visitor revenue, particularly from the overseas market. This evaluation was to prove particularly prophetic in the following 18 months. A more balanced revenue mix was needed to ensure delivery of the strategy. Nevertheless, along with the weaknesses there were undoubted strengths in the organisation, including a number of world-class qualities and, in particular, a committed and dedicated workforce.

A great deal of effort went into identifying the strategic goals shown in Figure 8.4 for the organisation, setting out what it intended to achieve. In formulating the goals it was recognised that there was a symbiosis between the business goals of operational excellence, customer and visitor satisfaction and financial performance, and the curatorial goals of conservation and education. For the organisation to function each goal was important.

Specific objectives were then identified in each of the critical success factors. These objectives are built into each annual operating plan throughout the whole organisation. These drive the objectives for palaces, departments, teams and individuals. A similar approach was taken with the guiding principles. Facilitated by John, all the management population was involved in deducing the specific behaviours that need to be present to underpin each guiding principle. These were then turned into a set of values by a cross-functional team.

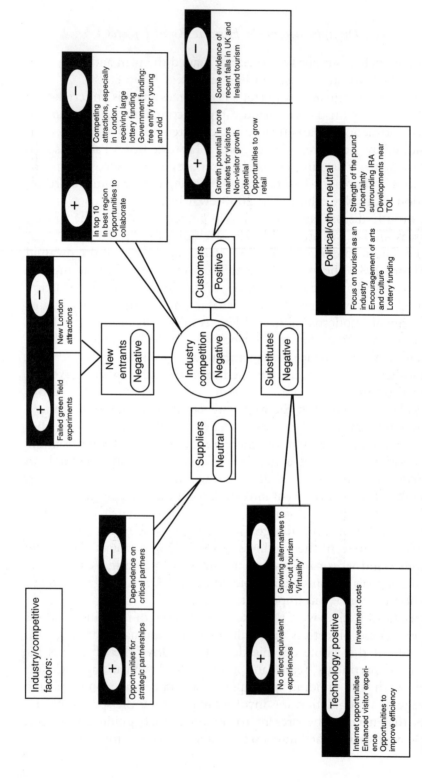

Figure 8.2 HRP faces a growing but increasingly competitive market and business environment

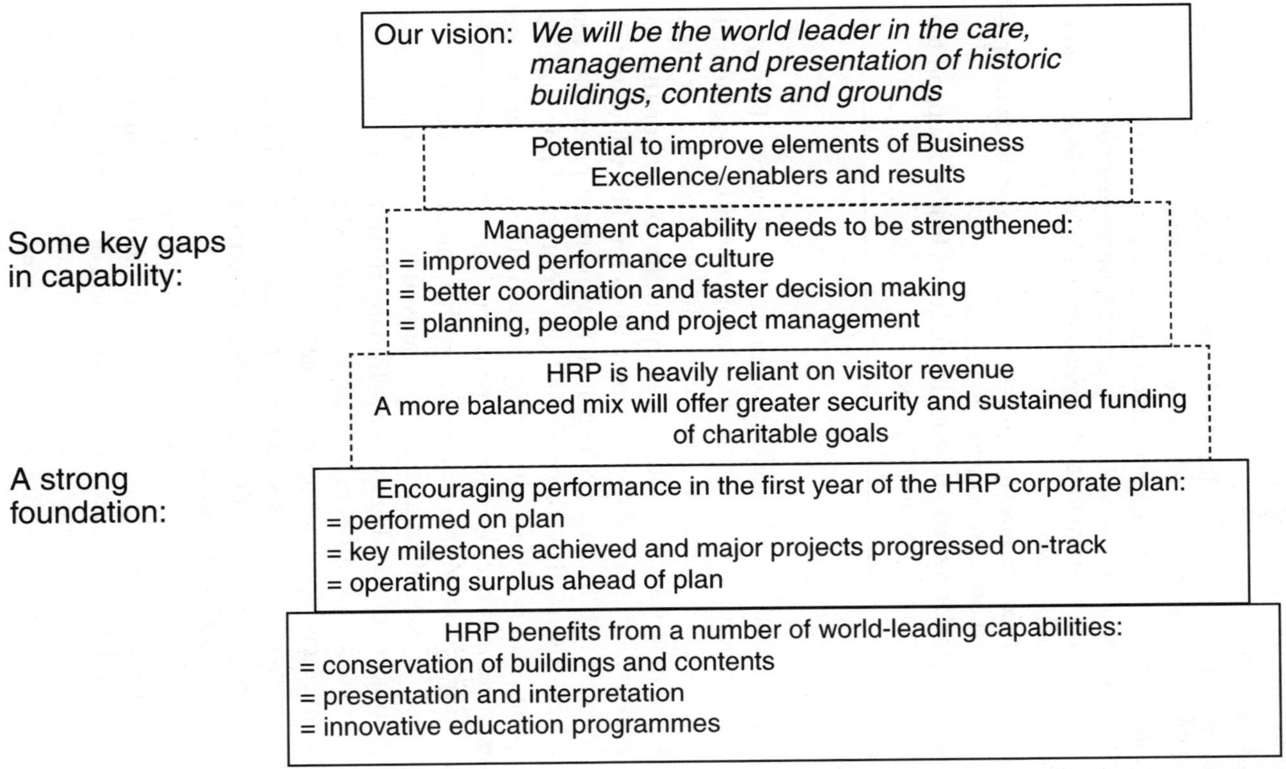

Our vision: *We will be the world leader in the care, management and presentation of historic buildings, contents and grounds*

Potential to improve elements of Business Excellence/enablers and results

Management capability needs to be strengthened:
= improved performance culture
= better coordination and faster decision making
= planning, people and project management

HRP is heavily reliant on visitor revenue
A more balanced mix will offer greater security and sustained funding of charitable goals

Encouraging performance in the first year of the HRP corporate plan:
= performed on plan
= key milestones achieved and major projects progressed on-track
= operating surplus ahead of plan

HRP benefits from a number of world-leading capabilities:
= conservation of buildings and contents
= presentation and interpretation
= innovative education programmes

Some key gaps in capability:

A strong foundation:

Figure 8.3 The current position is a strong foundation on which to build

---

The strategic plan is shaped by seven goals

- *Customer and visitor satisfaction:* to provide excellent visitor experience and customer service.
- *Preferred employer:* to retain, develop, motivate and attract the highest calibre people.
- *Conservation:* to excel in the development and practice of conserving the buildings, grounds and contents in our care.
- *Education:* to use the palaces and their history to inform and educate the public in the most inspiring and enjoyable manner.
- *Partnerships:* to maintain and develop mutually beneficial relationships with our partners.
- *Operational excellence:* to achieve and sustain standards comparable with best practice in everything we do.
- *Financial performance:* to generate sufficient funds to support the achievement of our vision and goals.

Figure 8.4

The cross-functional team's work was endorsed by directors. The values considered appropriate by the team for the organisation, together with additional values for managers, supervisors and directors are set out in Table 8.1. These values provide a framework for behaviour that will support the achievement of the purpose and vision. The values and the objectives are built into the performance management process so that all employees discuss their progress on both fronts, and plan development and improvements for the coming period. The values are set out here in some detail because they are pivotal to the achievement of the culture change programme, to implement the plan and get results.

A number of quantified targets were derived for each strategic goal (strategic objectives: see Figure 8.5). Initially these had one or more key performance indicators as measures. Currently a balanced scorecard is being developed, comprising both lead and lag measures. In addition the types of actions required to achieve the objectives, or tactics were set out. The goals objectives and tactics are all used in the Annual Operating Plan process.

Figure 8.6 shows the financial strategy, with income growing by just over £15 million during the plan period. The detailed back-up information shows this being achieved by a combination of revenue diversification (for example fundraising, off-site retail, functions and new events) and by modest growth in visitor and ancillary revenues.

Table 8.1 Historic Royal Palaces: Values

Guiding principle: exceed the expectations of our visitors, customers (internal and external) and partners

Value	*Definition*	*What we need*
Customer/ visitor service	Actively looks for ways to provide and improve levels of service to customers	Understands who the customer is in every situation. Displays a willingness to adapt and to make an extra effort to meet customer needs. Identifies visitor and customer needs through effective listening and questioning. Seeks to improve internal processes and procedures to meet present and anticipated customer needs Receives a customer request or complaint and remains accountable and committed to making sure it is dealt with. Acts to put complaints right immediately. Demonstrates accurate knowledge of their products and service, and what customers appreciate. Provides quality work on time to customers. Seeks feedback from customers, to understand satisfaction levels and to improve service provided. Is proactive and innovative with customers and visitors and responds to needs quickly, effectively and objectively.
Partnerships	Forms effective relationships with partners to HRP to achieve improved business results	Maintains regular contact with partners to identify and anticipate changing needs and service requirements. Identifies expectations of partners and works together to develop plans to meet those expectations. Works hard to find 'win–win' solutions to problems. Keeps promises.

/...

193

Table 8.1 (continued)

Guiding principle: pursue the highest level of quality, efficiency, service and innovation

Value	*Definition*	*What we need*
Continuous improvement	Willing to adapt and actively look for ways to improve personal and business performance	Demonstrates a desire to continuously improve personal, departmental and organisational performance. Embraces challenges, risk and change. Networks within and outside the organisation to identify best practice. Displays a willingness to use initiative. Focuses on finding solutions. Keeps an open mind on new ways of doing things. Supports actions and decisions that are good for the business. Copes with change and uncertainty and has a positive attitude to overcoming difficulties. Takes action to reduce inappropriate costs and increase profit. Has a positive 'can do' attitude.
Account-ability	Willingly accepts responsibility for own actions and the delivery of results on time and to agreed standards	Accepts personal responsibility for own work – 'If it is to be, it is up to me.' Solves problems without being asked. Shows a strong drive to achieve targets and results. Consistently meets targets and results on time, to the correct standard. Confronts shortfalls in performance.

Guiding principle: invest in, develop and value the abilities and commitment of our people

Value	*Definition*	*What we need*
Learning	Actively reviews experiences to learn from successes and mistakes and plans future behaviour accordingly	Formulates and agrees development plans with line manager. Seeks feedback from colleagues and customers on personal strengths and areas for improvement. Learns from experience and modifies his/her behaviour and approach. Accepts personal responsibility for learning.

Value	Definition	What we need
Learning		Contributes positively in Performance Review meetings. Actively applies new knowledge, skills and behaviours in their job to improve performance. Openly and proactively shares knowledge.
Team-working	Forms active relationships with colleagues to achieve business results	Works with colleagues rather than against them. Earns the respect of colleagues because of their positive contributions. Works effectively across departments and the organisation. Works hard to find 'win–win' solutions to problems. Keeps promises. Treats colleagues fairly, honestly, consistently and with decency. Contributes ideas to solve problems. Listens to and responds to questions and objections from colleagues. Takes time to enjoy successes in the company of those they work with.

Additional values for managers, supervisors and directors

Value	Definition	What we need
Leading by example	Demonstrates appropriate behaviour in line with HRP's Guiding Principles and Values	Actively demonstrates appropriate behaviour in line with HRP's Guiding Principles and Values. Practises what he/she preaches. Explains to staff the rationale for organisational decisions. Manages by walking about.
Providing a sense of direction	Develops within the team and individual staff a clear sense of purpose, direction and commitment	Shows a strong sense of direction by identifying where the team needs to be in the future. Develops a clear sense of purpose, vision and values within the team. Ensures that the team have clear goals, roles and procedures aligned to achieving the purpose, vision and values. Involves the team in creating this future direction and in identifying how it can be achieved.

/...

Table 8.1 (continued)

Value	Definition	What we need
Managing performance and development	Regularly agrees objectives with team and individuals and provides constructive feedback on a continuous basis	Agrees what is expected of staff in clear measurable terms (including objectives, standards and job profiles). Allows staff to do their job by delegating authority, accountability and the necessary resources. Assists staff to improve their performance through coaching and training. Acknowledges performance of staff through praise and constructive criticism. Actively uses HRP's Performance Development Review Process to appraise overall performance/ development needs to support further improvement and growth in the future. Recruits and manages staff against clear roles, standards and objectives. Deals effectively with 'under-performance'. Modifies personal style to involve staff and to gain their ownership of challenges.
Problem solving and decision making	Demonstrates a systematic approach to problem solving and displays sound judgement and decisiveness	Uses a range of decision-making techniques for solving more complex problems. Defines routine day-to-day problems. Analyses why routine day-to-day problems occur. Identifies alternative options and solutions. Weighs pros and cons, and impact of alternative options and solutions. Assesses implications and risk before making a decision.
Planning	Effectively plans and prioritises own work and the work of others	Produces detailed action plans to meet major business goals or objectives and to deliver agreed projects. Translates higher-level business goals into specific actions and responsibilities for the team.

Value	Definition	What we need
Planning		Makes time to plan and organise self and team for the short, medium and long term.
		Assesses the risks involved in implementing plans and generates strategies to manage these risks.
		Analyses the driving/restraining forces in delivering a plan and develops appropriate actions to strengthen/weaken these forces.
		Delivers against agreed plans and remains in control in difficult situations.
		Ensures projects are fully implemented according to agreed timescales.
		Coordinates planned activity with other parts of the organisation.
		Reviews and learns from experience.
Business improvement	Spends time working on the business and not just 'in' it	Focuses energy and effort on HRP's Strategic Objectives and key measures.
		Maintains awareness of developments and best practice in the marketplace and competitor activity.
		Reviews, maps, improves and redesigns processes to meet customer needs and to drive out non-value-adding activities.
		Develops standards, measurement systems and training initiatives to ensure effective operations of all key processes.

The extra revenues and improved cashflow are planned to fund maintenance/conservation programmes in the order of £4 million p.a. (uninflated) and major product improvement and capital conservation projects in the order of £6 million p.a. (uninflated). At the same time as this increased investment is being made, the cash balance is planned to increase from about £7.5 million in Years 1/2 of the plan to about £17 million by Year 5. Such a balance was deemed absolutely necessary for a non-subsidised heritage organisation of the scale of Historic Royal Palaces. We need to protect ourselves against a rainy day.

Strategic objectives and tactics balance commercial and charitable aims

- *Recognise and fulfil HRP's responsibilities under the Royal Charter.*
- *Run a commercially viable business in parallel with a charitable educational and conservation trust.*
- *For the commercial business:*
  - Realise significant benefits from implementing a new performance management culture.
  - Maintain the customer value proposition of the palaces as leading heritage tourism attractions.
  - Apply focused market communications and pricing strategies to sustain and selectively build visitor volume.
  - Maximise the revenue and margin from retailing and off-site franchises.
  - Balance other site-based revenue generation with the needs of conservation.
  - Maximise margin through premium pricing (events and functions) and efficient operations.
  - Develop strategic partnerships with key suppliers and complementary institutions.
- *For the charitable trust:*
  - Implement planned maintenance and conservation for buildings and contents to best-in-class standards.
  - Develop and implement an educational programme in partnership with educational institutions.
  - Further support charitable aims through fund-raising.
  - Develop and maintain core skills in conservation, education and fund-raising.

Figure 8.5

Events over the two years following production of the plan proved the thinking spot on. There just had not been enough time to build up reserves before foot and mouth and 11 September impacted.

Implementing the Strategic Plan

Of course it is only too easy to conduct a paper exercise to prepare a plan and then leave that plan on a shelf collecting dust. Of particular concern at Historic Royal Palaces was the state of the organisation's culture and

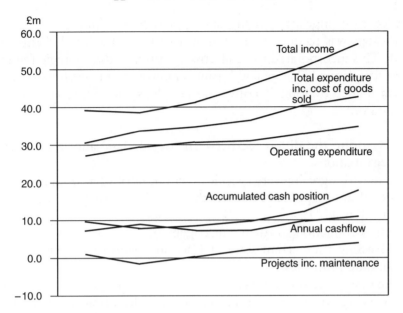

Figure 8.6 Margin improvement creates a firm financial foundation over the term of the plan: summary financial strategy with inflation

whether it was ready and able to begin implementation. Our conclusion was that it was not, and therefore we worked on designing a bespoke organisation business improvement process, a culture change programme. Such programmes aimed at changing thinking are not new, and are as valid for large commercial organisations as they are for small not for profit ones. Minoro Murofushi, the President and CEO of the giant ($US 120 billion turnover) Japanese Itochu trading corporation recognised this when he set up a 'corporate identity programme'. He discovered that even his company suffered from an overly conservative and bureaucratic culture, and that the organisation had to be returned to its roots as a risk taking, positive thinking and empowerment-based organisation if it was to compete in the modern world.

John worked with the Executive Board to develop a process that was directly related to the five-year plan. This is set out diagrammatically in Figure 8.7.

Executive Board workshops

Before encouraging change and renewal in the rest of HRP it was important to develop a common view of how the Leadership Team needed to change its thinking and approach. The purpose of these workshops was to develop a commitment to lead cultural change in HRP. This incorporated the collective creation of the strategic framework for planned change and business improvement. Each workshop was facilitated by John. To offer an example, some of the earlier work focused on:

- Exploring the difference between 'world class' and 'traditional' organisations.
- Explicitly agreeing very specific descriptions of what would be seen heard and experienced when the 'guiding principles' are being 'lived' in HRP.
- An introduction to change management.
- Assessing the current state of HRP in relation to its vision and guiding principles.
- Analysing the key issues currently restricting progress within HRP.
- Working to create a common positive dissatisfaction with the status quo and a collective commitment to lead the change for business improvement.
- Providing the necessary level of detailed description for the development of a supporting and integrated HR strategy.
- Explaining the concept and benefits of using competency definitions in business improvement and gaining agreement to develop HRP management competencies linked to the guiding principles.
- Improving the quality and effectiveness of team working within the Executive Board.

Leadership workshops

With this process stated in the Executive Board, the next step was to encourage a shift in thinking throughout HRP. The focus here was to allow people the opportunity to consider and understand the purpose, vision and guiding principles. The 'understanding' needed to go beyond understanding of the corporate need and intention. It was important to ask people to consider 'what this means for me, and what I need to do differently'. The key design principles were to:

- expose everyone to the same core ideas
- have a series of workshops to maintain momentum and slow down the 'sliding back to normal' syndrome

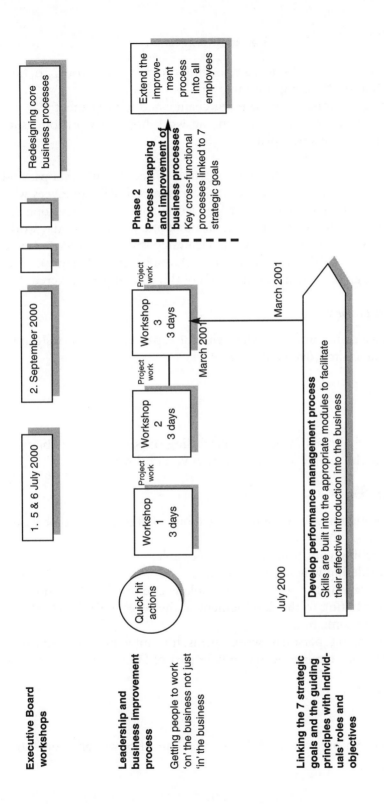

Figure 8.7 Leading business improvement at HRP

- create positive dissatisfaction and provide some tools to help people start the improvement process
- create a common language for change and improvement
- have 'project work' between the workshops to work on issues within the business plan.

Directors and managers went on three three-day workshops, and supervisors went on two three-day workshops. HRP employees who have not been on these events are still working through a development programme of five days. This is made up of one-day and half-day workshops. All the workshops were facilitated by John and Suzanne Rosenberg (HRP's Learning and Development Manager). The following gives a flavour of the kinds of things that were covered.

Overall purpose

To build a community of leaders with the capability to vigorously drive performance improvement in HRP.

Workshop 1

Purpose

To achieve a breakthrough in your feeling of power and capability to influence the people and the processes you deal with.

Outline content

- Exploring new ways of thinking about what is needed to be world leading.
- Stretching your belief of what is possible.
- Considering why we resist change.
- Investigating the power of our thinking and self-defeating thought.
- Contributing to the development of the core values for HRP.
- Having some fun.
- Developing personal action plans for implementing improved clarity of what is expected in your part of HRP.

Workshop 2

Purpose

To achieve a breakthrough in your feeling of power and capability to influence team performance and continuous business improvement.

Outline content

- Reviewing your project work and learning since Workshop 1.
- Exploring how to build trust and commitment.
- Using practical approaches with teams to encourage and support collective problem solving and improvement.
- Understanding the need for process management.
- Increased confidence on how to map and improve business processes.
- Having some fun.
- Developing a practical action plan for implementing improved performance in your part of HRP.

Workshop 3

Purpose

To achieve a shift in thinking and behaviour that develops an environment of shared responsibility and high performance within HRP.

Outline content

- Reviewing your project work and learning since Workshop 2.
- Developing a clearer perception of the rights and responsibilities of a manager.
- Creating an empowering environment for individuals.
- Improving confidence and capability to agree effective objectives.
- Developing simple frameworks for giving and receiving constructive feedback.
- Exploring how to improve your effectiveness as a coach.
- Understanding the new HRP Performance Management System.
- Having some fun.
- Developing a practical action plan for creating an environment of shared responsibility and high performance within HRP.

These workshops were vital to allow people the opportunity to choose to commit to the future HRP. They were also central to providing some tools to help them create this future state (positive dissatisfaction and knowing how to improve things). They were highly valued.

This is illustrated in the following summary of how the 145 directors, managers and supervisors evaluated the workshops.

Relevance (0 = not at all relevant, 10 = very relevant)

How relevant has this workshop been to you as a Manager in HRP?
    Average score: 8.89

Renewing and focusing thoughts on effective leadership (0 = not helpful, 10 = very helpful)

How well has this workshop helped to focus and renew your thoughts on effective leadership practices?
    Average score: 8.96

Beneficial investment (0 = a poor investment, 10 = a valuable investment)

How do you rate this as an investment of company money?
    Average score: 8.79

The all-employee workshops are still running. However, the feedback from the first one-day events, attended by 310 people, was:

Relevance (0 = not at all relevant, 10 = very relevant.)

How relevant has this Workshop been to you as a member of HRP?
    Average score: 7.9

Commitment (0 =not at all committed, 10 = highly committed)

How committed are you to working together to HRP to become a world-leading organisation?
    Average score: 9.2

Beneficial investment (0 = a poor investment, 10 = a valuable investment)

How do you rate this as an investment of company money?
    Average score: 7.6

While this programme was key to creating a groundswell of energy, a clear focus was necessary to prevent the spawning of a plethora of initiatives. Equally, a strategy is useless unless it has a mechanism to translate it into specific actions. Furthermore, we needed a means to jointly review performance and agree development needs. A cross-functional project team was developed to build a recommended process for this.

The team was led by Suzanne Rosenberg and comprised 12 members from 11 different departments or teams. It did not have any directors on it. This in itself was a marked culture change, and was a deliberate choice. Our aim was to foster increased ownership, to demonstrate that important processes can be developed using a different approach from the 'normal' HRP method, and to provide an

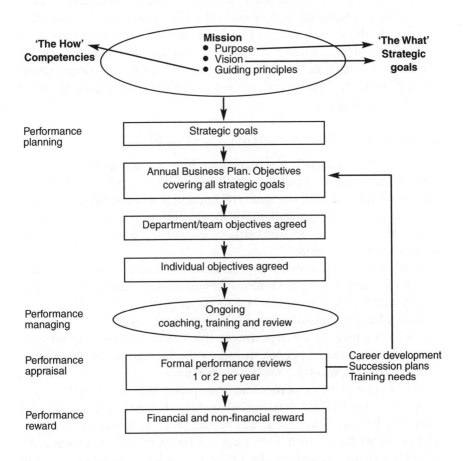

Figure 8.8 Performance management process

205

example of what can be achieved by a team of aligned and attuned people. The team did an excellent job. Their recommendations were implemented without any significant alterations.

Process improvement projects

Once we had worked at getting attitudinal shift in place and a lot of 'quick win' improvements, the next challenge was to create a mechanism for systematically leading change and improvement within HRP. In effect, this meant the creation of a 'company standard' for efficiently and effectively 'working on' the business. The aim was to tackle cross-functional problems and processes, the ones that are usually left in the 'too hard to do' box. An initial team was trained in the use of the approach and the associated skills in February and March 2002, and started work on the first project, involving other members of HRP to identify the causes and find practical and effective solutions. This will become a permanent part of HRP's culture, and a key vehicle for continually renewing 'how the work works'. Unless an organisation has a planned and resourced process for continuous improvement, it is unlikely to happen.

Resolving organisation structure anomalies

In 1999 the organisation structure at Historic Royal Palaces was a typical 'hierarchical' structure, as shown in Figure 8.9. A thorough review of the structure was undertaken, and it was concluded that the basic structure was appropriate for the organisation but that a number of anomalies had to be addressed to ensure it was capable of delivering the five-year plan.

Not readily apparent from the structure design was an underperforming and overstaffed Human Resources department. This needed speedy action: the remoteness and inefficiency of this department were sources of major dissatisfaction in the listening exercise. Unfortunately, given the culture of the department this could only be dealt with by releasing a number of people, including the Director (who went first). The department was then relabelled 'Personnel and Development' and now has a complement of nine staff, compared with 18 before.

Another overstaffed department was the Finance section, under a very able Finance Director. It was agreed that the number of staff was inappropriate for a £40 million turnover business and a plan was instigated to reduce numbers. In order to achieve this change other

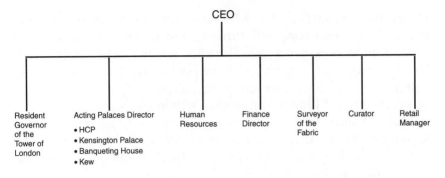

Figure 8.9 The former organisational structure

changes had to be made to the way the organisation operated. For example the use of procurement cards and a rationalisation of suppliers significantly reduced the number of invoices to be paid. This process is part of the continuous improvement approach that has been adopted and is therefore ongoing.

A clear anomaly from the structure was the positioning of the retail department, a vital contributor to the organisation's revenues. The Retail Manager attended the Executive Board meetings. To all intents and purposes she was a Director; she just did not have the title. This was immediately rectified by her promotion, and along with it the promotion organisationally of her department.

A replacement was sought to replace the Acting Palaces Director. The interview process was completely different from any previously used at HRP, and was based on an assessment centre methodology. This included:

- competency-based interview (which replaced the antiquated 'talk me through your career' type interview)
- presentation
- ability tests (numerical and verbal reasoning)
- occupational personality questionnaire.

An internal candidate won through.

The organisation lacked marketing expertise at board level. Since anticipating and satisfying customers' requirements (a classic definition of marketing) was at the root of the new approach, this needed to be remedied. A headhunting exercise revealed a number of excellent candidates, and through use of the new assessment centre approach we eventually identified a new Marketing Director. This Director drew together various people involved in marketing scattered around the palaces into one cohesive department. He also set up the critical fundraising section within his department.

Small changes were made to reporting lines, for example the Banqueting House became the responsibility of the Governor of the Tower of London because of its geographical closeness and opportunity for joint working on functions business.

The final structural change was implemented in 2001. Again this change, perhaps the biggest in organisational terms, the merging of the Surveyor of the Fabric and Curatorial Departments, was totally in line with the five-year plan and the need it identified for a continuous improvement capability. Following a great deal of thinking and consultation, Alan decided a merger was necessary into a new Conservation Department. He concluded that such a merger would strengthen the key conservation effort which had been split between the two existing departments. The other benefits to having one team devoted to Conservation and Education included:

- Facilitate communication and the sharing of knowledge and skills between all members of HRP staff with conservation experience.
- Focus accountability for leading the delivery of our Conservation and Education strategic goals.
- Improve cross-functional team working between conservation staff and other departments in HRP.
- Ensure HRP conservation has a world-leading voice in global heritage.
- Eliminate the confusion sometimes caused by overlapping responsibilities, thereby allowing staff to deliver a more efficient service to both internal and external customers.
- Ensure one single conservation voice for HRP when dealing with outside partners and agencies such as English Heritage.
- Provide conservation with a critical mass of staff and resources: the combined department became the third largest in people terms within HRP (after Palaces and Tower).
- Strengthen the relationship with other key partners such as the Royal Armouries and the Royal Collection.
- Ensure that vital development, interpretation, research and project

work for improving the offer to visitors is coordinated and planned by one main specialist department.

The merger was wholeheartedly endorsed by the Trustees, who believed that a single team of conservation experts, working towards a common goal, was an essential prerequisite for the delivery of a world leading conservation and education service.

Once the decision had been taken and the two Directors had been notified (one was to leave, the other one accepted a different role), the recruitment exercise was started. Because of the sensitivity of the issue Alan personally saw each of the managers and supervisors from both departments to explain the decision. He also communicated the change to all staff via personal letters and in personal presentations and spoke with key partners, such as English Heritage, to ensure their involvement in the process. A new Conservation Director took up his position in September 2001, and a key task will be to ensure the successful practical merger between the two departments.

Results of the Timeless Management approach at Historic Royal Palaces

Having a strategic plan and great implementation processes are all very well but what about results?

Prior to 11 September 2001 and the horrific terrorism acts in New York and Washington, Historic Royal Palaces was some £2 million ahead of its strategic plan cash balance. This result was of course a function of other activity within the organisation rather than an achievement in its own right.

Two other measurement areas – our customers and our people – illustrate the impact of our Timeless Management approach.

First, customers. During the summer of 2001 a comprehensive visitor survey programme was undertaken by an independent specialist organisation, MEW. The key measures of value for money, helpfulness and friendliness of staff, and enjoyment of visit were all going in the right direction! (See Figure 8.10.)

As to the staff, a large scale employee climate survey was organised, a more formal version of the earlier listening exercise. This too was undertaken by an independent specialist company. The exercise was (coincidentally) timed for the end of September 2001, just after the vile terrorist acts in America.

Eighty-eight per cent of Historic Royal Palaces staff participated

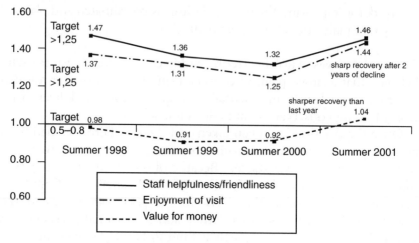

The scores are based on an industry-standard 5-point scale.
Excellent +2; Good +1; Just OK 0; Poor –1; Very poor –2

Figure 8.10 Historic Royal Palaces Key Performance Indicators

in the survey. The key results were that overall, there were high levels of satisfaction amongst employees of Historic Royal Palaces:

- Satisfaction was high (78 per cent) among employees at HRP. The intensity of satisfaction was high when compared to the All Surveys benchmark and top quartile.
- Motivation was high (71 per cent) among employees at HRP. Again, the intensity of motivation was high when compared to the All Surveys benchmark and top quartile.

(The Benchmark is an average of all the surveys carried out by the survey company in the past. The top quartile is an average of the results from the top 25 per cent of companies. These benchmarks are based on results from a cross-section of sectors worldwide, including utilities, manufacturing, pharmaceutical, government and retail.)

Conclusion

From the above information it was concluded that the organisation was making significant progress against its strategic plan objectives. Then, pow! First the organisation was hit by the impact of the foot and mouth epidemic (resulting in 8 per cent fewer visitors), then the double whammy of 11 September. If you really want to make God laugh, show him your plans!

Timeless Management, and in particular the approach that had been used to manage the organisation, will be sorely tested in the coming months. Has there been significant change as an organisation, at least enough to be able to respond rapidly to the adverse impact of 11 September? The next chapter provides an early evaluation.

9 The response to the terrorism of 11 September 2001

Every calamity is a spur and valuable hint.
Emerson, 1860

The worse the passage the more welcome the port.
Fuller, 1732

Greater dooms win greater destinies.
Heraclitus, c. 500 BC

To be brave in misfortune is to be worthy of manhood;
To be wise in misfortune is to conquer fate.
Agnes Repplier, 1924

Fire is the test of gold; adversity of strong men.
Seneca, 1st century AD

On the afternoon of 11 September 2001 Alan was working in an office in Kensington Palace when Pam Heard, his personal secretary, called with the grim news of the first attack. A television was brought to the office and with a small number of colleagues he watched the unfolding events in total amazement and horror. Within minutes it was clear that these dreadful attacks would have an almost immediate adverse impact on Historic Royal Palaces.

Of course the Palaces' problems were minuscule in the overall scheme of things, and particularly when compared with the devastating human problems on the other side of the Atlantic. The scale and tragedy of the New York and Pentagon attacks were numbing. The barbaric act had a depressing effect on all normal people throughout the world. Nevertheless, during his drive home Alan realised he had to try set these feelings aside. He used the hour with the radio off to set a framework for action, and by the time he reached home he had the bones of what turned out to be these five leadership assumptions:

213

- Not to be deflected from the strategic plan by terrorists but recognise it would take longer to achieve.
- The dreadful action provided HRP staff and the organisation with an opportunity to show leadership and act differently from other affected companies.
- This would be a temporary problem and there was a long term future for Historic Royal Palaces.
- The organisation would find ways to turn negative into positive.
- A determination that the organisation would emerge from the period of difficulty as a stronger organisation.

A key aspiration emerged from these assumptions and the belief the organisation had in its people: an intent that not one of the staff should be made redundant as a result of the terrorist attack. It is very easy in times of business difficulty to treat people purely as an overhead and simply cut them to cut cost. Many much larger organisations than Historic Royal Palaces adopted this approach post 11 September. But how could the Executive Team? In leadership development programmes and 'journey' workshops they had consistently told their people how important they were. It would have been unforgivable and a betrayal of the teams' beliefs to cull their colleagues at the first difficult moment. And yet they were setting themselves an almost impossible aim since staff costs represented about 55 per cent of the organisation's overhead base.

Having established the leadership assumptions, the Executive Team at Historic Royal Palaces embarked on another impossible, though necessary, task: identifying the problem by predicting the length and scale of the impact of 11 September on Historic Royal Palaces. First it was important to understand the impact of other major events on visitor numbers. Coincidentally regression analysis (another useful tool to learn from the past) had recently been undertaken by MBA students from the Said Business School of Oxford University. The regression analysis plotted over a 20-year period attendances at the Tower of London and Hampton Court Palace, the main revenue-generating operations within the organisation. The students identified and illustrated on charts the impact of a number of negative and positive events on the attendances, including the Gulf and Falkland Wars. These charts are set out in Figures 9.1 and 9.2.

After 11 September, attendances were tracked daily and, as feared, the immediate impact anticipated actually materialised (although

Oxford MBA Work

Tower of London Visitor Number Residual (1980–1990)

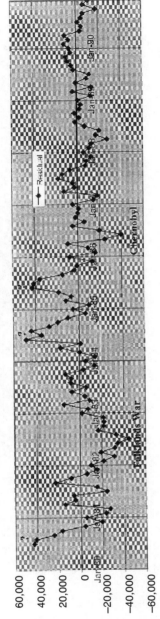

Tower of London Visitor Number Residual (1990–2000)

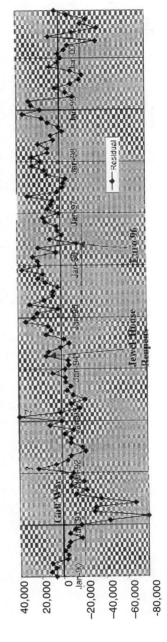

Figure 9.1

Oxford MBA Work

Hampton Court Palace Visitor Number Residual (1980–1990)

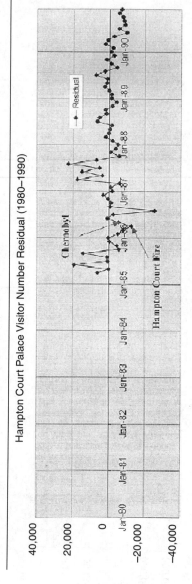

Hampton Court Palace Visitor Number Residual (1990–2000)

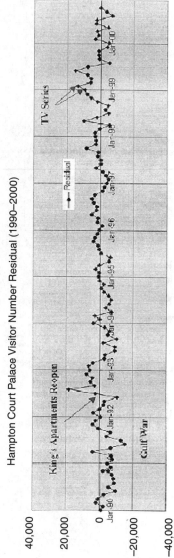

Figure 9.2

slightly better than their projections) at about 32 per cent down for the Tower of London and Kensington Palace and 17 per cent down at Hampton Court Palace. With this data in mind the team reminded themselves of the visitor mix and particularly the percentage of visitors from foreign countries (see Table 9.1).

Table 9.1 Research on the visitor numbers

	Tower of London %	Hampton Court Palace %
UK	23	53
USA	40	19
Europe	24	16
Other	13	12

Other important factors were also noted, such as the immediate impact on the airline industry worldwide. The response by the USA and its coalition partners was likely to be a long drawn-out exercise, and the fact that planes were used as weapons in the attack was likely to have a medium-term impact on the propensity of people to fly.

From these exercises the team then quantified the problem and made a number of working predictions, which included:

- The US incidents might be different in scale from the Gulf and Falklands Wars, but the Oxford University work supported the leadership assumption that the effect would be temporary.
- Because of the immensity of the US attacks it was considered Historic Royal Palaces could be impacted over a three-year period (much longer than previous 'wars').
- For the Tower of London and Kensington Palace a 40 per cent adverse attendance impact (based on the number of US visitors to each property) was predicted, and 22 per cent adverse impact for Hampton Court Palace (which attracts fewer visitors from North America).

The resultant financial impact was likely to be a cumulative cash deficit in year 2004/5 of £18.9 million: quite a large figure for an organisation with a £40 million annual turnover. It was realised that there was only one thing right about the projections: they were wrong! Nevertheless, there had to be a starting point and it was felt the problem had at least been quantified and the causes were only too well known.

A top level Executive Team exercise to determine an appropriate action plan was undertaken. Five options to bridge the anticipated cash gap were identified:

- Do nothing, hope matters will improve.
- Cut project and operating costs (known benefit, because in HRP's control).
- Increase revenues, including fundraising (unknown benefit not in HRP's control).
- Borrow. Because of the unique status of Historic Royal Palaces this would require government permission.
- Request government assistance.

The second to the fifth options were not mutually exclusive.

The desire not to make permanent staff members redundant was reaffirmed, as it was believed this would ensure that when the organisation did emerge from this temporary period it would do so stronger (one of the leadership assumptions). Nevertheless, a number of areas were identified where, with lower anticipated visitor numbers, operating costs could be reduced. Maintenance was not included, as maintaining the historic properties was seen as a core duty.

In addition to operating cost savings, it was recognised that it would be necessary to postpone (not cancel) the organisation's ambitious capital project programme for two years (the anticipated length of the cash problem). However, priority was given to proceed with the Tower Environs Scheme, a major project to improve the environs and approaches to the Tower of London, since this was already receiving significant grant aid from the Heritage Lottery Fund and Port of London Partnership. Nevertheless, Historic Royal Palaces had a £4.5 million contribution to make. It was also considered sensible to put in place a borrowing facility to tide over the organisation and to cover any further income erosion. Extra effort would be needed on fundraising (there was an important upcoming meeting with Sir Paul Getty) and to generate other income. However, at that stage these could not be relied on and so were excluded from the plan.

A further conclusion reached was that it would be necessary to do things differently and do different things – a way of thinking that was being developed as part of the leadership development programme, and totally in synch with Timeless Management. For example, the planning process was changed immediately and a new fast track annual operating

plan preparation format and timetable agreed. This reduced the preparation time of the plan from over four months to one month. It was
subsequently discovered that the shorter timescale was much preferred
by departmental teams, and it will be adopted for all future plans. This
was just one of many examples of turning a negative into a positive.

Within two weeks of the terrorist incidents, the Executive Team had
prepared a plan which they were united on. This plan was presented to
the Trustees and it received unanimous endorsement.

The next important step was to start involving all HRP staff.
Normally involvement would have started earlier, but because of the
speed of the impact of 11 September action had to be very fast, which
inevitably meant a top down approach. In common with all civilised
human beings, the people at the palaces were incredibly affected by
the terrorist actions. Coupled with a sense of outrage and concern at
world events was a more local worry: how would the knock on effects
impact on Historic Royal Palaces and their jobs? They could see on a
daily basis the lower numbers of visitors, and they well understood the
implications. But before these colleagues could be reassured it was
necessary to come up with some answers, and to do this required focus
on the problem and the development of at least an initial action plan.

By the third week after the terrorist attacks all staff had received a
personal letter from Alan and had been invited to attend presentations
given by him. During these presentations, which were well attended,
the hard truths were explained, together with the proposed response.
The leadership assumptions and the critical role of all staff was
explained. Contributions were requested from staff, and their involvement solicited in refining the 'top down' plan into a 16-month 'annual'
operating plan.

The response was magnificent. Colleagues contributed by submitting
ideas for consideration (some of these were implemented immediately,
such as an innovative discount scheme aimed at attracting domestic
visitors), by being involved in and delivering their detailed plans in
record time (the plans themselves were full of new ideas and new ways
of doing things) and by their general support and positive attitude.

The resultant fast track plan was approved by Trustees on 28
November, and again this plan was presented to the staff by way of
personal presentations, backed up by hard copies for those who could
not attend. Very regular updates were given by means of email, the
staff newsletter *Palaces Pulse*, but most importantly, as far as possible
by directors and managers 'walking the talk'.

While the action plans were being prepared, other actions were taking place simultaneously. A crucial meeting with Sir Paul Getty was held at Hampton Court Palace, involving the Earl of Airlie and Field Marshal Lord Inge (Chairman and Deputy Chairman respectively of the Trustees). At this meeting they requested the assistance of Sir Paul to part-fund the Tower Environs Scheme in order to enable it to proceed. After a further meeting at the Tower of London with Sir Paul's advisor, a message was received during the Trustees' meeting on 28 November that Sir Paul would donate £4.5 million to Historic Royal Palaces, a most generous and helpful contribution. This was also a good example of turning a negative into a positive – it is doubtful whether a donation on this scale would have been sought if not for the extreme financial impact of 11 September.

Unfortunately, initially it was not possible to get the same prompt decision from our request to government to put in place a borrowing facility, despite having lined up two private sector banks. Work in partnership with the DCMS to convince the Treasury to change the rules to enable such a facility is ongoing.

So what has been the effect of all this on Historic Royal Palaces? Let us first look at the impact on visitor numbers (see Figure 9.3). Actual percentage variances compared with the previous year are shown on this chart to December 2001, and projections thereafter. We will be updating these charts on our web site in order to make the case study live for Timeless Management readers who want to follow the fortunes of the palaces.

As can be seen, a significant drop in visitors took place immediately after 11 September. The impact was immediate, as the main income streams (from day visitors) are cash-based, and key overseas visitor groups (particularly from North America) cancelled their travel plans. In Historic Royal Palaces, cash is king too! This is not to downplay the importance of our worthy conservation and education goals, it is merely a non-subsidised body facing reality. The impact of the actions that were taken on the key cash line in terms of cost reduction, project deferral and fundraising is shown on Figure 9.4.

This chart shows, perversely, that despite a projected 32 per cent fall in visitor numbers and a consequent significant drop in revenue, the cash projection was forecast to be £3.2 million (about 42 per cent) *ahead* of the original five-year plan cash target at the end of March 2002. Furthermore, rather than the organisation going into a cash deficit position of £18.9 million in the year 2004/5 (as was forecast

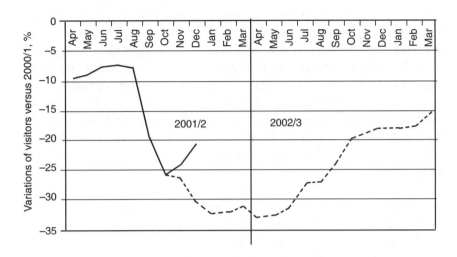

Figure 9.3 Monthly variances of visitors in 2001/2 and 2002/3 compared with 2000/1 as the base

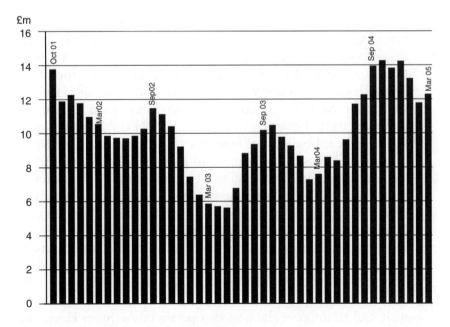

Figure 9.4 HRP monthly cashflow forecast

immediately after 11 September), this chart shows a cash reserve at this time of about £12 million. It was still expected that HRP would achieve this position without making one permanent member of staff redundant, although it would be necessary to defer some capital projects. This result was not achieved by prestidigitation, but rather more boringly and simply: by the application of Timeless Management.

In addition to the critically important planned and routine conservation and maintenance work and to the 'normal' workload, the organisation has embraced the need to do different things and do things differently. As far as business-related activity, the following are merely examples of hundreds of new ideas and approaches that have been adopted:

- In Marketing: in January 2002 the Tower hosted the worldwide launch of 'UKOK', the British Tourist Authority's major come back to Britain campaign; at Kensington Palace and the Tower in February 2002 the US prime time television show *Good Morning America* was hosted; Hampton Court Palace was the location in January and February 2002 for a major new feature film *Cromwell and Fairfax*, generating publicity and location fees; from March 2002 the Tower of London starred in a new eight-programme Channel 4 television series; also in March 2002 came the screening of a BBC *Meet the Ancestors* special programme instigated by and featuring a Palaces Curator, Jonathon Foyle; follow up of staff suggestions to run a two for one ticket promotion and exit promotions to cross-refer visitors to other palaces and incentivise schoolchildren who visit with schools to return with their families.
- In Visitor Services: visitor access to Kensington Palace was improved from the Spring of 2002 by the opening of the 'Golden Gates' (where bouquets of flowers were left in memory of Diana, Princess of Wales); development of a new Historic Royal Palaces web site by a cross-functional team including the sale of tickets to the palaces on the Internet; new exhibitions at Kensington Palace (Royal Wedding Dresses) the Tower of London (Prisoners) and Hampton Court Palace (Royal Stamp Collection).
- In Operational terms: implementing staff ideas to effect operational change and save costs, such as redeploying Admissions staff at the Tower; working in partnership with the unions to introduce more modern and competitive working practices and procedures; working with staff to improve the way we operate in the Jewel House and

White Tower; developing an in-house team to deliver staff development and continuous improvement training workshops.

- In Conservation; undertaking a research project for the European Commission into the measurement of damage to historic textiles and thereby attracting European funding; Dave Howell, the Conservation Scientist, is developing a new technique to colour enhance part of one of the Abraham tapestries located in the Great Hall at Hampton Court Palace to show how tapestries must have looked when new (this idea resulted from a discussion between staff attending a training day).

- In Fundraising: securing private sponsorship funding valued at about £800,000 to provide a spectacular fountain to commemorate the Queen's Golden Jubilee; launching a corporate membership scheme at the Tower of London and a Friends scheme at Hampton Court; securing sponsorship from Nestlé for interpretation events; working collaboratively with the organisation Arts and Business.

- In Retail: opening a new satellite shop in Guildford over the 2001/02 Christmas/New Year period; developing the licensing programme by targeting 'anchor' licensees in areas such as china, silverware and soft furnishings; exploring department store concession trading; establishing an e-commerce operation including gifts by post (translating traditional mail order offers onto modern technology).

The performance improvement of people across the palaces has stepped up at least one gear since 11 September. So the future is anticipated with confidence, and there is every prospect that the leadership assumptions made immediately post 11 September, of a stronger organisation emerging from a period of adversity, will be realised. If this does happen it will be due entirely to the creativity, energy, commitment and collaboration of Historic Royal Palaces staff. This is not a meaningless tribute to staff, of the type that is to be found in some company Annual Reports, just because it is expected. Not only is it true, it is the essence of this book; people deliver results.

But it is early days yet. History teaches us that hubris and nemesis can be closely linked so we must never become complacent. There is so much more to be done.

You will be able to judge for yourself over time how successful (or otherwise) the organisation and its people have been by logging on to the Timeless Management web site.

Timeless Management lives on at www.timelessmanagement.com

In writing this book we not only wanted to set out an approach to getting things done through people which we passionately believed in, but we wanted to present an array of practical techniques so that others interested in our beliefs could try them themselves. Drawing together and applying the five timeless traits should provide a comprehensive strategy for personal and organisational improvement.

In this last part of the book we have set out, briefly, a case study showing how the Timeless Management concept has been applied in Historic Royal Palaces. Of course, this represents only a brief period of time, particularly in the context of the long history of the palaces. Who is to say that the concept really works over time? When you buy the book, what comfort have you that the concept is not already obsolescent?

Of course, we can give no guarantees; we can only guess shrewdly into the future. But we can keep the case study going through the use of modern technology. This may not be pioneering stuff but it is at least an example of doing things differently. So from June 2002, and quarterly thereafter, updates on the progress or otherwise of Timeless Management at the Historic Royal Palaces will be provided on the Timeless Management web site, www.timelessmanagement.com.

For those of you who prefer to stop with the book, thank you for your time. We hope it works for you. For those who are keen to see how we progress, we look forward to seeing you in cyberspace!

We earnestly encourage you to give us your views on Timeless Management. This will help us to achieve our goal of continuous improvement. So please write to us at Alan Coppin and John Barratt, Apartment 39, Hampton Court Palace, Surrey KT8 9AU, or email us on our Timeless Management web site.

Selected bibliography

Ackroyd, Peter (1999) *The Life of Thomas More*, Vintage.

Ashley, Maurice (1973) *The Life and Times of William I*, Weidenfeld & Nicholson.

Brimacombe, Peter (2000) *All the Queen's Men: The World of Elizabeth I*, Sutton Publishing.

Byham, William C. with Cox, Jeff (1994) *Heroz*, Ballantine Books.

Byham, William C. with Cox, Jeff (1999) *Zapp! The Lightning of Empowerment*, Random House Business Books.

Dauphinais, G. W. and Price, Colin (1998) *Straight from the CEO*, Nicolas Brealey.

de Bono, Edward (1998) *Simplicity*, Viking/Penguin.

Drucker, Peter F. (1955/2001) *The Practice of Management*, Butterworth-Heinemann.

Drucker, Peter F. (1967) *Managing for Results*, Pan.

Drucker, Peter F. (1990/1999) *Managing the Non-Profit Organisation*, Butterworth-Heinemann.

Fortescue, Sir John (1925) *Wellington*, London.

Fraser, Antonia (1997) *Oliver Cromwell: Our Chief of Men*, Arrow.

Fraser, Antonia (1979) *King Charles II*, Weidenfeld and Nicholson (reprinted by Arrow 1998).

Haigh, Christopher (1988, 1998) *Elizabeth I, Profiles in Power*, Pearson Education.

Handy, Charles (1997) *The Hungry Spirit*, Hutchinson.

Heller, Robert (1998) *In Search of European Excellence*, HarperCollins.

Hibbert, Christopher (1998) *Wellington: A Personal History*, HarperCollins.

Hibbert, Christopher (1999) *George III: A Personal History*, Penguin.

Hill, Christopher (2000) *God's Englishmen: Oliver Cromwell and the English Revolution*, Penguin.

Kline, Nancy (1999) *Time to Think*, Ward Lock.

Koch, Richard (1997) *The 80:20 Principle*, Nicolas Brealey.

Longford, Elizabeth (2001) *Wellington*, Abacus.

Marius, Richard (1984) *Thomas More*, Alfred A. Knopf.

Mintzberg, Henry, Ahlstrand, Bruce and Lampel, Joseph (1998) *Strategy Safari*, Free Press.

Nicholson, Nigel (2000) *Managing the Human Animal*, Texere.

Porter, Roy (2000) *Enlightenment: Britain and the Creation of the Modern World*, Penguin.

Roberts, Andrew (2001) *Napoleon and Wellington*, Weidenfeld & Nicholson.

Smith, Douglas K. (1996) *Taking Charge of Change*, Addison-Wesley.

Starkey, David (2000) *Elizabeth: Apprenticeship*, Chatto and Windus.

Strachey, Lytton (1987) *The Illustrated Queen Victoria*, Bloomsbury.

Tinniswood, Adrian (2001) *His Invention So Fertile: A Life of Sir Christopher Wren*, Jonathan Cape.

Townsend, Robert (1984) *Further Up the Organisation*, Michael Joseph.

Turner, Colin (1995) *The Eureka Principle*, Element.

Weintraub, Stanley (1997) *Albert, Uncrowned King*, John Murray.

White, Michael (1997) *Isaac Newton: The Last Sorcerer*, Fourth Estate.

Index